'I worked with the Kissells  in a very encouraging ministry and f[...]
Bishop David Pytches, founde[...]

'In my late teens and early [...]
hour or two with the Kis[...]
was always the same – I'd leave their home [...] [...]
spirit. This special book from Mary Kissell will likely have
the very same effect on you. It's a refreshing read in the
company of someone who loves Jesus dearly, and has
learned so much from following Him. As Mary tells her own
life story, there are many life lessons for us along the way –
on loving people well, trusting God through suffering, and
living in dependence on the Holy Spirit of God. There is
faith, grace and wisdom on every page. Enjoy!'
Matt Redman, songwriter and worship leader

'A remarkable pilgrimage to read and many lessons to learn
from it'.
*Debby Wright, Senior Pastor at Trent Vineyard with her husband
John. Together they are National Directors of Vineyard Churches
UK and Ireland*

'There is a compelling depth and integrity about Mary
Kissell's first book. With highly perceptive and some
humorous insights she charts a remarkable story of God's
faithfulness in her own life, her marriage and ministry with
husband Barry, and their extended family. For this reviewer,
who has known and worked with them for many years, the
chapter "Give!" goes to the heart of her journey. "Each day
we wake receivers of the grace God extends to us. The fact
is, we can never out-give God." Here is a beautifully written

book to nourish the soul, raise the level of faith and pass on to others.'

'A unique Christian biography! Unique, because Mary Kissell not only charts the good times in her life but also the pains, struggles and disappointments. But she does more! She shows us, her readers, the way through the hard times and the benefits of feeding on the positives. This is a must-read gem!'

Before the Days Draw In

My ordinary journey towards an
extraordinary God

Mary Kissell

**instant
apostle**

First published in Great Britain in 2018

Instant Apostle
The Barn
1 Watford House Lane
Watford
Herts
WD17 1BJ

British Library Cataloguing-in-Publication Data

A catalogue record for this book is available from the British Library

This book and all other Instant Apostle books are available
from Instant Apostle:

Website: www.instantapostle.com
E-mail: info@instantapostle.com

ISBN 978-1-909728-91-2

Printed in Great Britain

Dedication

To Barry and our beloved family

Acknowledgements

LES MOIR: Who casually suggested, 'Why don't you write a couple of chapters and send them to me?'

DAVE ROBERTS: Who chewed it over and pushed doors for me.

THE INSTANT APOSTLE TEAM: Who took the risk to publish.

SHEILA JACOBS: Whose keen eye and inspired suggestions propelled me to the finishing post.

NIGEL SCOTLAND: Who patiently talked me through theological issues.

NOONIE SPENCER: Who without complaint unravelled the technological problems that beset me and, with Jonnie, gave unstinting support.

BARRY: Who is the best husband and companion ever.

Contents

Preface 13

Introduction 15

Chapter 1: Beginnings 25

Chapter 2: Finding God in a Cornish Kitchen 37

Chapter 3: Forgiveness 49

Chapter 4: Herbs and Spices 61

Chapter 5: Return to Nursing 73

Chapter 6: The Muffins 83

Chapter 7: Trip to New Zealand 95

Chapter 8: Give! 107

Chapter 9: Move to London 117

Chapter 10: Time of Testing 129

Chapter 11: The Wonders 141

Biography 153

Preface

Psalm 78 begs us to take seriously our responsibility to 'tell the next generation' what God has done. A dream challenged me to do this.

To do justice to the enormous package of God's grace, I have pulled out key moments that I look back on as being pivotal in shaping my faith. Most important for me was the decision to get up one hour earlier to learn to pray. A simple table in a Cornish kitchen proved to be a place of transformation.

Every step of faith taken towards Almighty God results in the unexpected. My story includes a career I would never have chosen, moves to places I was reluctant to go, painful acceptance of my own ungodliness, the adoption of a traumatised family, and family ill-health. Above all, my eyes have been opened to the wonders of the kingdom of God, the inexpressible generosity of our heavenly Father and His longing to be intimately involved in all the details of our lives. The ultimate victory is that He accepts us with all our failings and works lovingly to make us more than we could ever humanly be.

I have sought through this book to convey this.

Introduction

I was born in October, as were my husband Barry, my mother Lydia, my granddaughter, my niece, my sister-in-law and two of my daughters-in-law. October is the family month; it is also my month.

I love October, the sharpness in the air, the glorious colours, squirrels darting around frantically in their search for acorns, knowing time is at a premium. Bright berries of late summer are beginning to fade, and everywhere there are warning signs of one season giving way to another. Sunsets are dramatic, the light more golden, and evenings creep in stealthily, robbing us of long hours outdoors.

When I was younger, the challenge, with friends, was to resist covering our legs with stockings before the beginning of October. I never could. Last year's jumpers and tartan skirts were hauled out of drawers and wardrobes in defence against the chill. October is a month to hold on to for as long as possible, to be outdoors, to walk and savour the goodness of the year.

One night I had a dream that I had moved to a home called October Cottage. It was very vivid.

'What can it mean?' I asked Barry.

'Perhaps we will move in the future. I like the name October Cottage,' he replied. Moving did not resonate with me. I was enjoying the feeling of being settled, having moved to London a few years previously. Upping sticks again was not foremost on my agenda. Perhaps there was another meaning.

It is funny with dreams or words that come like lightning bolts into the heart; their message has lasting impact, even growing in intensity with time, but they are not always clearly understood. I remember waking one night in 2006, having had such an experience. I sat up in bed, woke Barry and told him earnestly, 'The snows are coming!'

'Ugh?'

'The snows are coming,' I repeated.

He turned over without comment. Two years later and hardly a flake had fallen, yet economically the country was sliding into the biggest winter for nearly a century. The financial crisis of 2008 rocked the country, bringing it into a time so bleak it did indeed feel as if the snows had come. I have learned to wait and listen to the voice of the heart; this is where God speaks and unveils the true meaning of these messages. God does not make it difficult for us. He has made known to us through the Scriptures that He wants to communicate with us. Dreams are one way that He does this; the Holy Spirit helps us in our interpretations, by teaching us to see beyond the natural. These insights are available to anyone who is eager to hear and see.

Prophecy is simply learning to see beyond what we can see. Perhaps this is why Jesus said we must 'become like little children' (Matthew 18:3). Very small children act intuitively and sometimes recklessly. They rely on an 'inner knowing' about the world around them, sometimes referred to as a sixth sense, before they have language to express themselves and minds able to reason logically from the knowledge they have stored up. As language and knowledge increase, they switch to a greater reliance on reason.

Dreams and their interpretation are like two pieces of a jigsaw puzzle that fit together. When the Spirit brings revelation, there is almost a discernible *click*, with a 'That's it!' as the two pieces of the puzzle come together. God speaks to us in dreams to unfold His purposes, to give us insight and warnings and also to relay His promises. He has spoken to me in dreams throughout my life. Sometimes the meaning is immediately clear, but other times I have to leave it and wait. Then, quite unexpectedly, the *click* that releases the meaning comes. I had to wait for the meaning of the dream to move to 'October Cottage'.

I heard the *click* I had been waiting for while driving on the A40 into London, focusing on nothing but my destination. A *click* and a flash came together: October Cottage was not so much a tangible place I would move to, but a season I was about to enter. God keeps a diary recording His times and seasons. Only when it involves us does He begin to prepare us for them, closing down much of what went before and putting in our hearts new possibilities for the future.

I felt quietly excited about this season, believing it would be good, rich and the culmination of all that had gone before. 'Good' is what uniquely stamps everything that is from God. It is His trademark, the hallmark that assures His workmanship. The quality of the brand is beyond contradiction because of His name. Everything that comes from Him is good. He wants us to be convinced of this, stating this truth, again and again: 'The LORD is good and his love endures for ever' (Psalm 100:5). What He does is good and what He has created is good. Goodness flows from the heart of God. Corruption of this truth is a key strategy of the devil. Through deception, he confuses and entices us over the boundary line that separates good from evil, thus blurring the edges. God is jealous of His brand name: 'Woe to those who call evil good' (Isaiah 5:20).

Do you also look at creation – the sky, sea, birds, animals, plants and trees that evoke a response of wonder, and think how strange it is that we experience such delight? Even in their starkness, the branches of trees, divested of their leaves, silhouetted against a winter sky, bring pleasure to my soul. Why? I believe our hearts simply resonate with God's approval of what He has made. Surveying creation I imagine Him with notebook in hand going through His checklist and ticking them all: 'Good!' And on day six having a quick glance around, making His final summing up. It is recorded, 'God saw all that he had made, and it was *very good*' (Genesis 1:31, my italics). We grunt our agreement when our hearts too are moved. What we see is good. We glimpse, at times, a world unsullied by destructive invasion, reflecting the nature of the Creator.

When the rich young man fell at the feet of Jesus and asked, 'Good teacher ... what must I do to inherit eternal life?' Jesus responded with a question: 'Why do you call me good? ... No one is good – except God alone' (Mark 10:18). He was pushing the young man towards the truth about Himself, that He and the Father were one and that is why he called Him good.

Knowing that this new season I was about to enter was instigated by God, I also knew that my confidence was not misplaced.

October holds the fullness of the year, following all the months that have gone before – a hard winter, faithful sowing, the nurture of plant growth and then the gathering of fruit bringing the year to the completion of its cycle. October is a time to sit back and reflect and enjoy nature's final symphony of colour before the cycle begins all over again. This is what I proposed to do. It was like a house move; to enter into it fully I would need to trawl through all that constituted my present life and decide what would be taken with me and what I should leave behind.

Seasons, of course, do not arrive abruptly – summer one day, autumn the next – there is a gradual transition, often taking place unseen. Then, there is a barely discernible sharpness, evoking the comment, 'I felt a tinge of autumn in the air today.' Suddenly our eyes are open to the decline of summer, the need to reach for a cardigan in the evening, the shorter days. Inward adjustment is made to accommodate the change, a sense of anticipation mixed with nostalgia. It is unsettling.

When we prepared to move to London, Barry and I entered the loft for the first time in years. It had been so easy to climb the ladder, open the trapdoor and just push yet another bundle through. In the darkness it was impossible to see what had accumulated over the twenty-nine years that we had lived in our home. With the move date firmly in our diaries, it was time to climb the ladder again and have a really good look. After we had trawled through bags and bags, there were just a few items that we thought would be worth salvaging. They had been part of our lives for many years, hardly acknowledged, yet important in defining who we were as people. The London home we were moving to was a large Victorian house with five bedrooms and a basement. However, it was only a temporary residence while the last of our fledgling family prepared for the next stage in their lives.

After three years Barry and I were rattling around and it was decided that it was time to move to a much smaller home of more permanence. We settled on a two-bedroom flat, which had no extra storage space. Radical pruning was required this time. Our visits to the council tip were a daily pilgrimage until we were left with what would truly represent our new life in the present. I did not miss a thing that I had had to leave behind.

So, entering a new season, it was time to repeat the process by making an assessment of what I would need to take with me to form a lasting framework for my future life.

I had entered my sixth decade when I had the dream. There was a lot to trawl through. The Lord, who was always pushing the Jewish community towards the future, gave them orders to look back, not with regret, but with thanksgiving. They were to remember what He had done. 'Remember that you were slaves in Egypt and that the LORD your God brought you out of there with a mighty hand and an outstretched arm' (Deuteronomy 5:15). There were lessons that were pivotal to the shaping of them as a nation, milestones that altered the course of their history and difficult times when their faith was tested. God told them to talk among themselves, recounting these times, to pass these stories on to their children. 'Tell of all his wonderful acts' (Psalm 105:2); 'Tell the next generation ... [what] he has done' (Psalm 78:4).

I often imagine that our lives are like a book, recording everything that has happened to us up to the present day. They record every event and season that we have lived through. I have lived through spring, summer and part of autumn in my life cycle. There is much to reflect on and to remember and to pass on to my children and grandchildren, before the days draw in and I miss my opportunity.

God seems to be a great believer in writing. Over the years He had His scribes put in writing words that would last forever. The prophets were commanded to write it down. Treasuries of words were passed down for generations, with relevance in the presence matching that of the past. I like recording things in words. Lists, scraps of paper tucked behind bottles of olive oil in my kitchen, and inside the covers of books, regularly flutter to the floor during the course of the day. My favourite means of expression is to write in notebooks. More notebooks than

21

the number of my years are stacked in drawers and regularly counted by my grandson Daniel.

Before beginning a career in nursing, in 1962, I worked for two years in a bank. I was surprised to discover that a relative of mine had valuable silver stacked away in the vaults. There it sat for years until her death, when it was spirited away to her beneficiaries. Just imagine, I was literally yards away from a treasure trove that I did not even have the opportunity to glimpse before it disappeared forever. I want my family to glimpse the good things the Lord has done for me before they too are beyond their reach.

It is time for me to open up my notebooks, to discover afresh the life lessons that have lasting significance for me. Apparently my writing is incomprehensible, which I find very difficult to believe, but I must take my family's word for it and read through the scribblings of years, to extract what has been most valuable to me to pass on to them. These truths impressed upon me during key moments of my life will provide furnishings for me too, in the coming seasons, and bear witness to God's faithfulness in all circumstances.

God, who has a unique destiny for each one of us, prepares us by teaching us what we need to know to fulfil it. Peter learned a hard lesson when he lacked the courage to acknowledge he was a disciple of Jesus. Denying this most precious of friendships scarred his heart deeply. After His resurrection, Jesus reinstated him as a much-loved friend and gave him the means to rise above his fears, the Holy Spirit. Peter is the first disciple to boldly proclaim the message of the gospel of Jesus Christ to those assembled in Jerusalem at the Pentecost celebration, as recorded in Acts chapter 2. My own personal weaknesses have scarred me too. By finding healing through the Spirit's power, these same weaknesses have equipped me to live more fully and more joyfully and to know God in a deep and personal way. They continue to hold lessons for me in the present and are the treasury I want to pass on to my beloved family – and to you, the reader.

Chapter 1
Beginnings

An attic flat in Northwood, Middlesex (that county that has no place on a map, but nevertheless is a postal address!), became our first home. It was tiny, with a small kitchen divided by a curtain from a sitting room, just large enough for an armchair, a coffee table and a chaise longue that stood under the small window overlooking the railway line beyond. Our bed was squeezed under the sloping eaves of a second room and meant Barry had to climb in first to settle, and remind himself not to rise quickly to avoid banging his head! We shared a bathroom with our neighbours on the second floor. It was in Northwood that Barry had embarked on his theological training and I worked in the local hospital.

These were good years. We made many lasting friendships and above all were introduced to the transforming power of the Holy Spirit. It was with sadness that we all went our separate ways at the end of the final college term. Barry was among the last to find a curacy. We had hoped to join a wonderful couple in Bromley, Kent. Tiny Palmer was the tallest person I had ever met. His wife was the granddaughter of General Booth, the founder of the Salvation Army. Despite their advanced years, they had a fiery vision for renewal. We loved spending time with them. It was therefore with great disappointment that we were told that the bishop had stepped in to say, 'Time's up.' It was time for them to enjoy retirement while we were placed in the alarming situation of having nowhere to go.

Our anxiety grew as the term drew near to its conclusion. Then, when all hope of a placement had faded, Barry came home to report he had had the strangest encounter with a young man from Cornwall who had been sent by his rector to look for a curate to join him in Camborne. It was the most unorthodox situation, not to mention bizarre! He arrived at the college unannounced, and bumped into Barry, who was consequently invited to travel down to Cornwall to see if this might work for him, and the rector, of course. So it was that we found ourselves travelling to the far South-West to push another door. To our relief, this one opened.

However, we had to vacate our flat two weeks before the scheduled move. Tim Watson, a friend, who was curate of Emmanuel, Northwood, and a former student at the London College of Divinity, where Barry trained, kindly invited us to move into his home. He was going away and was happy for us to stay in his absence. Our short time in Tim's home was not without incident. We had hardly settled in when there was a knock on the door; it was a parishioner asking for Tim. He was crestfallen when he heard he was away.

'But he always looks after my dog and my parrot!' he exclaimed.

In a rash moment, I said, 'Oh, that's fine. I'll look after them.'

A shiny black Labrador and a grey parrot clinging to a swinging perch in his cage were duly handed over. The dog was wonderful. I have always loved having a dog around. But the parrot tested my patience to the extreme. His owner had clearly invested a lot of time in teaching him key phrases, which he practised over and over again in perfectly enunciated English, mimicking his owner's voice. 'Hello, Tono,' he would repeat throughout the day, interspersed with loud screeches and demands. Exclamations of indignation followed if his demands were not met. Something would obviously need to be done about Tono. It was with triumph that I discovered I could quiet him down if I threw a large towel over his cage. He hated it, and muttered irritably within his darkened world until I relented and removed the towel. Then he let out a victorious screech and began his endless tirade again. We never did become lasting friends. I happily handed him back to his owner before we prepared for our move.

Meanwhile Barry had hired a large van to transport our belongings down to Cornwall. Another college friend shared the driving with him and helped unpack our furniture, which included the chaise longue. At the time it was covered in a fabric of woven tapestry. It had a dip in the middle, where many had sat. Worn in places, the horsehair stuffing poked through the threads of the weave. Our landlady had asked us if we would like to take it with us when we moved. We would. It weathered four subsequent moves and is still with us, fifty years later. Barry, not a trained upholsterer, did a reasonable job of recovering it when the stuffing surfaced in great tufts after our second move. He had to pull out the horsehair and replace it with a thick sheet of foam. When we later moved to London, we found a professional upholsterer who restored it to its original form. Back went horsehair! A thick blue and gold tapestry fabric that I found in a local store was perfect for its covering. This piece of furniture symbolised our life together, when foundations were being laid. We were yet to be repaired!

Foundations are what count. They mark the beginning of what has not yet been realised. They are the starting point of what I look back to as being a journey begun. The patriarchs of Israel, as recorded in the Old Testament, set out on journeys where they had memorable encounters with the Lord that became foundational to their faith. To remind themselves of these times, they set up stones or pillars for others to see. Jacob, after long years of labour for his father-in-law, Laban, eventually broke away to begin a new life with his family. Laban, aware that he was about to lose everything, followed in hot pursuit. He caught up with him at Gilead. It was terrifying for Jacob! But God was on the case. In a dream he gave Laban a warning, 'Be careful not to say anything to Jacob, either good or bad' (Genesis 31:24). In other words, 'Keep your mouth shut!' He could not resist a bit of a grumble about the way Jacob had sneaked off. Jacob too had quite a backlog of grievances to get off his chest and out it came. There was no turning back now. Laban got the message.

He humbles himself. 'Come now, let's make a covenant, you and I, and let it serve as a witness between us' (Genesis 31:44). In other words, they agreed to make peace.

Jacob takes a stone and sets it up as a pillar. His family brought other stones and piled them in a heap next to it. The stones were to stand as a lasting memorial to a covenant made, to words of reconciliation, a moment that changed the destiny of a whole family. Jacob was able to journey on; the shroud of resentment had lifted. God's word directing him during one of the most difficult times of his life had given him the courage to break away. He had simply said 'Go ... and I will be with you' (Genesis 31:3). The completion of that particular chapter in Jacob's life was witnessed by a stone set up by the roadside. God had spoken similar words to us. We knew we had to go and in time we also knew that He was with us. There was no stone for us, but a battered piece of furniture that has been with us from the beginning.

If inanimate objects could talk they would have amazing stories to tell. Our chaise longue has been silently present throughout our married life. I believe if it could speak it would bear testimony to the outworking of my relationship with the Lord from my early days in Northwood where it stood under the window overlooking the railway embankment to my eventual move to London. In my imagination it stands as a witness to the power of a covenant with God that has stood the test of time. It seemed significant that this particular witness should be uprooted and carried to the far South-West to continue its watchful vigil.

Moving to Cornwall was the first move of our married life. I felt that we had been spirited there. I did not want to go. My vision for the future had directed me to Bromley and now I found myself in a strange county nearly 300 miles away. In fact, to make sure I did not escape, I was at the furthest end of this rocky peninsula, in an old mining town. On the day we set out it was pouring with rain. The windscreen wipers that had worked hard to clear our vision gave up the task as we neared the Tamar Bridge. We limped our way through Plymouth and across the bridge into Cornwall. Here the rain stopped and gave way to a thick grey mist that enveloped us all the way to Camborne. The church of St Martin's loomed above an ancient graveyard, with aged tombstones sticking out at angles like rugged teeth. Our new home was opposite the church.

We arrived at dusk only to discover that the small terraced cottage that would be our home for the next four years needed shilling coins to feed the electricity meter. We did not have one! Our neighbour, two doors up, graciously handed us a coin. This enabled us to boil a kettle, after which, to save power, we made up the bed and slumped into exhausted sleep.

Gritting my teeth and getting on with the job has always been my way of coping with challenging situations. That was what I did in the first few weeks of adjusting to change. I settled in as well I could, but my inner life was in turmoil.

Before moving down to Cornwall, my Christian life had been largely fuelled by meetings I had attended during a new move of the Holy Spirit. Sporadic manifestations of the power of God often accompanied by 'speaking in tongues' were causing shockwaves in churches. Freshly energised church leaders were stepping out with renewed courage and holding healing services with the laying on of hands. In addition to hymns accompanied by the organ, new worship songs were being introduced, led by groups using guitars and other instruments. There was a ferment of change with the inevitable protests from nervous traditionalists.

Prior to this, I had yawned my way through a few prayer meetings while believing in my heart that, God being God, there must be something more dynamic than I was experiencing. Some of my friends had been Christians for years and could flick through their Bibles with ease, pulling out relevant verses for all occasions. I had read Mark's Gospel at school, with a view not to gaining spiritual nourishment, but to passing an exam. It was therefore with great excitement that I stumbled upon a passage in Scripture: 'In the same way, the Spirit helps us in our weakness. We do not know what we ought to pray for, but the Spirit himself intercedes for us through wordless groans' (Romans 8:26).

I read and reread this. Could this possibly be the 'gift of tongues' I had heard about? It really resonated with me, a sporadic, unenthusiastic pray-er, who had got stuck in my spiritual development. God's timing, as always, was impeccable. Within days of reading that verse, Barry received a phone call inviting us to join a small gathering of people at St Andrew's vicarage in the neighbouring town of Chorleywood. Edgar Trout, an inspired preacher, would be speaking that afternoon. There would be opportunity for those who wanted to receive the Holy Spirit to be prayed for with the laying on of hands.

Although eager to receive this mystery gift of the Holy Spirit, I was also nervous. Edgar ministered with great authority, and prayed for us all. I had hoped for an immediate manifestation of holy power. I had to wait. It came a few days later, one evening when I made another stab at reading the Bible. This time I alighted on the book of Acts, and began reading the first chapter. The words started leaping from the pages with heart-impacting significance. I read the whole book in one sitting and for the first time felt the tangible presence of the Holy Spirit. Later I found myself 'speaking in tongues' when I ventured to pray. Aspects of this mystery were beginning to make sense. 'For anyone who speaks in a tongue does not speak to people but to God. Indeed, no one understands them; they utter mysteries by the Spirit' (1 Corinthians 14:2). It certainly felt that way.

Life was exciting for us after that. Barry was sitting in the library of the theological college where he was training for the Anglican ministry when he was suddenly filled with the Holy Spirit and began praising the Lord in tongues. Our friends were daily receiving the gift. We gathered together frequently to pray and share testimonies and have meals together. It was wonderful, a real awakening. I felt more spiritually alive than I had ever felt. In between working at Mount Vernon Hospital, I spent a lot of time attending church meetings. Billy Graham, the American evangelist, held a big rally at Earls Court in London in 1966, attended by hundreds of people who arrived in coachloads to hear his message of salvation. I was able to get a seat on one of the coaches leaving locally. The power of Billy's message touched me deeply. It was a rich season for me.

All this came to an abrupt end as the summer term finished. Those with whom we had intimately shared our lives had dispersed to different parts of the country, and we moved to Camborne.

The contrast to the previous few months could not have been greater. Renewal had not yet reached St Martin's and my feeling was that I was on my own. There were no prayer meetings. I had no friends nearby. The realisation dawned that most of what I had received spiritually was second-hand. Others had fed me, nurtured me and filled my spiritual water jar. Now, here I was in a place without any familiar supports. I had never felt so empty and isolated. What I was yet to learn was that this was a good place to be. God puts us in deserts in order that we will hunger and thirst for Him. To survive, I was going to have to forage for my spiritual sustenance. I decided to get up one hour earlier. I would start to put a daily discipline of prayer as my priority for each day, something I had never done before.

It is strange that we can spend a lifetime sitting through church services and actually not really pray. I had spent years doing just that. Of course, I mumbled my way along through the prayers set out in the Book of Common Prayer, but without any thought that there could be a meaningful connection with the Lord. It actually created a huge tension in my head. I felt self-righteous and as detached from God as ever. What I really liked doing was singing, and church gave me that opportunity. In my teens I joined a choir local to my home in Lymington, Hampshire. This proved to be life-changing, not because of the singing, but because a middle-aged lady, also in the choir, opened up her home after the evening service. She thought a discussion group might be helpful in developing the spiritual life of interested church members. I liked discussions as well as singing and went along. It was there that I met Barry.

Barry had hitchhiked across the globe from New Zealand with his friend Brian. They were making their way to Jerusalem, where Barry's parents were living at the time. (His father had a post with UNESCO.) Barry was eager to spend an extended period of time there to explore the city. Before setting out again, he worked in a refugee camp in Jordan. Friends of Barry's parents who had spent time in New Zealand had returned to England and had settled in Pennington, a small village outside Lymington, where I lived. They generously gave Barry lodgings and he started to attend the church that I too had joined.

Barry had become a Christian in Wellington, just weeks before leaving New Zealand to go on his travels. A huge rally had been organised in one of the big rugby stadiums and Barry was invited to go with some friends. Billy Graham was the speaker. The message he gave was compelling and Barry found himself surging forward in response to the call to make a commitment to Christ. Despite no previous interest in Christianity, he found himself utterly convinced in that moment and, as he left his seat to go to the front of the stadium for prayer, he felt God was also calling him to the ministry. It was a lot to take on board in one day! He left New Zealand to work it all out.

An unusual group of people gathered for the weekly discussion at the home in Pennington, and I remember nothing about the topics we covered, but we all had a lot to say. I found myself sitting next to Barry and found his comments amusing. He seemed to turn up a lot after that, not to the discussion group but to places where I happened to be. Our second son, Tim, on hearing the account of the early days of our relationship, commented that his father's tactics would have today been described as those of a stalker!

Barry made the decision to stay in England to pursue the call he had received in Wellington. After taking the requisite number of entry exams, he began his training at the London College of Divinity, Northwood, a theological college for men training for the Anglican ministry. We married one year later in 1965 and I too moved to Northwood where I resumed my nursing career until our first son was born. With God guiding our destinies, it was always going to be an adventure. We could not have predicted the places that would become pivotal in shaping us and maturing us in our faith. When Barry had completed his training, the choice was taken out of our hands by circumstances. We journeyed to the South-West. Our real training was about to begin.

Chapter 2
Finding God in a Cornish Kitchen

Every journey has to start somewhere. Mine began at the kitchen table of our small Cornish home. It was autumn and the dampness that typified the far west of this rugged county sank deep into the cottage walls.

The kitchen was the warmest room; at least, it normally was. An old black range was set against the furthest wall. It became one of our greatest challenges during our four years in Cornwall: a friend when it burned brightly, and a foe when it defied attempts to sustain heat.

Coming down the stairs in the morning I would hold my breath anxiously, wondering whether it had made it through the night. Banking it up the evening before to keep a residual glow that could be coaxed into flame the next morning was a hit-or-miss affair. This stove was so temperamental. On a bad day, the depressing news was carried to Barry who was still savouring a few extra minutes of sleep. He would rise reluctantly to start the grim task of relighting it. This necessitated laying newspaper on the floor and removing all the old coke before relaying kindling and starting again. Billows of grey smoke would fill the room, from a chimney that had not been swept for years. The smoke dissipated as the back door was opened to the Atlantic winds, but by that time I was freezing and my spiritual temperature had also plummeted. Such days were not conducive to the early beginnings of my prayer life, but did increase my awareness of good and evil. The discovery of barbecue lighter bricks, quite new then, revolutionised the management of our main source of heat and convinced me that the Lord was on my side!

On a good day I was welcomed by a pleasant, mood-enhancing heat. After making a mug of tea, I would settle on the kitchen stool armed with my Bible, notebook, pen and a piece of paper. Distraction is a popular strategy of the devil to divert us away from prayer. I fell for it time and time again. Armed with scrap paper I sought to thwart his tactics by capturing wandering thoughts that would direct me to supermarket shelves for items I needed to buy, phone calls I should later make and letters that had to be responded to. Once discharged on to the paper, I would again address myself to the matter in hand. I still stuff my Bible with bits of paper for this purpose, although my concentration has improved over the years.

As a child I would accompany my mother to the grocer's shop where she would purchase the items she needed to stock up the larder. There were no supermarkets then. She would simply hand a list to the grocer who would disappear behind the counter to assemble the items required. He would wrap them in brown paper before the transaction was completed and we would walk home. My early days in my prayer place at the kitchen table were like a visit to the grocer's shop. I would recite my list of prayer requests. Often the same prayers were repeated day after day in the hope that frequent repetition would broker the deal I hoped for. I am sure God stifled a yawn as I came yet again to repeat what I had mentioned the day before. He remained silent, no doubt hoping that I would too. I ploughed on, getting a measure of relief through the discharge of my anxious thoughts.

Anxiety had been building up for some time. My early years had been dominated by my uncertain relationship with my mother. It made me feel insecure. I was not yet ready to look at those early chapters. Barry was concerned with the level of stress I was carrying daily. One evening when he headed for the church hall to meet with the young people who formed the youth club, I trawled the bookshelves for a concordance. I hoped that I would find some biblical reference to anxiety. I did: 'Do not be anxious about anything, but in every situation, by prayer and petition, with thanksgiving, present your requests to God. And the peace of God, which transcends all understanding, will guard your hearts and minds in Christ Jesus' (Philippians 4:6-7).

It was a prayer package; pray, give thanks and receive. It was worth a try. I poured out everything that was currently causing me inner distress. In response to the next instruction I began to thank God as a gesture of gratitude that He had heard me and was taking action. A lightning bolt of power hit me, flooding me with a peace I had never experienced before. It travelled from my head right through to my feet. I was consumed by it. It was immobilising. I sat while wave upon wave of peace flooded through me. It was wonderful and also beyond understanding.

That day, Barry returned and took one look at me and said, 'You look totally different!' He was amazed at the transformation. My encounter also transformed my daily prayer time. I felt I had at last made a real connection with the Lord.

Above everything else, I yearned to know the daily presence of the Holy Spirit. My prayer routine would need to be altered. The silence of a new day stills the senses to absorb the truth of the presence of God; it confirms the truth found in James 4:8 that if we draw near to God He will draw near to us. My chatter had dulled my awareness. He had been there from the moment I had entered the kitchen. I could relate to Him as a friend, not merely as a dispenser of my requests. Our relationship was two-way. He opened my eyes to new concepts I could never have humanly understood. I in turn felt able to voice my concerns, believing that He would take action that would result in the very best.

I love the fact that the Holy Spirit is as unpredictable as the wind, reflecting the heart of God. We cannot anticipate how He will work to unravel the tangled situations we find ourselves in. He just asks us to trust Him and let Him get on with it. I was going to have to do that more and more. Knowing that He was with me gave me spiritual security.

Feeling the presence of God has been important to me. I have had many rebukes about this. A common belief is that we should merely take the fact of His presence by faith without expecting to actually feel anything. Just as in our human relationships, especially with those closest to us, we have moments of hardly acknowledging their presence, yet we are assured of their love because of the trust we have established over time. But most precious are those times of intimacy, when the warmth of the relationship is kindled again, strengthening our bonds with each other. Without those times the relationship thins. This is mirrored in our relationship with the Lord. When we feel the closeness of His Spirit, like a warm embrace, our faith is strengthened. It leads us into spontaneous worship. We are confident to unburden the smallest details of our earthly struggles, knowing that He understands and will take a fatherly responsibility for them.

A young woman once came to see me, weighed down by the stresses of life. She told her story. It was a history of failed relationships, sadness and disappointments. The burden she carried was huge. What could I answer? I felt the Lord say, 'Don't say anything, just wait.' I told her we were just going to sit together and I would ask the Holy Spirit to come. We waited. I prayed silently and urgently. Gradually I began to sense His presence descending upon us like a cloud of holiness. I hoped she was sensing the same.

'Are you feeling anything?' I ventured to ask.

'Oh yes,' she said.

'Well, let's wait a bit longer.'

We waited for a long time, both enshrouded in this wonderful presence. Later I was able to say to her, 'That is the power available to you.' I did not need to say anything else. She knew where she could get the help she needed to rise above her troubles. Feeling the presence of God gave her the assurance she needed. He was the great power to help her and she only had to ask.

Meeting with God is about a relationship, not a formula. Knowing that He is with us allows a communication that is both ways. Enoch stands with the great heroes of faith listed in Hebrews chapter 11. Little is said about him. I wondered, 'What on earth did he do?' I found a reference to him made hundreds of years before in the book of Genesis. Apparently his claim to fame was that he walked with God. 'Was that it?' Apparently, yes! Companionship with God is what He treasures above all else. 'Enoch walked faithfully with God; then he was no more, because God took him away' (Genesis 5:24).

Our prayers flow out of a confidence in that relationship. We can tell Him anything. He whispers back through that voice in the heart that gives an inner knowing that He has spoken. When we are distanced from Him, we lose that. I was reminded of the patience of a fisherman, casting his line. He watches for the bob of the float to alert him to a catch. He then gently plays the fish in. The fish swims off and is repeatedly reeled in closer and closer to shore. Eventually it is landed and is in the hand of the fisherman. The Lord does the same, reeling us in until we are as close as we can be. This is the place of whispers. John the disciple made it his mission to get as close to Jesus as possible, leaning with his head against Him. He heard things that the other disciples were unable to hear. This is evident in the Gospel of John and the book of Revelation.

I have learned that the Spirit speaks in whispers, glimpses and nudges. Being close to the Lord enables us to make a response to these gentle communications. Simple leadings can have profound outcomes. I'm reminded of an incident some years later when returning home one afternoon, I had an impulse to visit my neighbour. I really wanted to put my feet up with a cup of tea after a busy day, but the thought persisted. I decided to pursue it. I called. She came to the door, gasping, 'Thank goodness you have come. I prayed that someone would call.' She was pale and shaken, having fallen off a stool. Her injured arm was causing her a lot of pain. It would have been so easy to ignore the nudge to call.

Promptings from the Spirit will guide us in our prayers. People whom we have not thought of for a long time will come to mind. As we pray for them, small insights will guide us and sometimes we are rewarded by hearing news confirming the rightness of those Spirit leadings.

In Camborne we seemed to be fighting a battle in defence of the Spirit's relevance. We refused to be moved.

Our belief and hope in the Holy Spirit were unshakeable. Barry proclaimed the truth of this holy power and ministered it through the laying on of hands, whenever he had an opportunity. On two different occasions local ministers turned up on our doorstep, armed with doctrinal evidence to challenge Barry's heretical position. It was hurtful but unconvincing. Once tasted, the presence of God that seeps into the soul is beyond contradiction. How could we possibly deny what we had witnessed and experienced? Christian communities were coming alive as they opened their lives to this wonderful source of power. We ourselves were recipients. Jesus' promise to pour out His Spirit on all flesh was bringing hope to us. We knew it and testified to it.

It is impossible to draw near to God without the challenge to change. He is the embodiment of holiness and the light that shines from Him highlights areas that have evaded His healing power. When I was first exposed to this power I could not stop shaking. It felt like an earthquake in my soul. Later, when I made intentional steps to develop a prayer time, it was inevitable that the pain of my past that was fracturing my inner life would again come under God's loving scrutiny. I could no longer avoid it. To go forward I had also to go back to allow it to surface. It was uncomfortable and terrifying. Spiritual healing is like that. Those who have suffered in a similar way even take the step of avoiding going to church where they lose the battle to push down what they have not been able to face. It is a relief now for people to know that the expression of painful emotions is to be expected in a place where the Holy Spirit is welcomed. Emotions are attached to painful experiences. Their expression frequently heralds the freeing of that attachment to the past. Churches that openly welcome the ministry of the Holy Spirit are safe places for people to come.

Cornwall became that safe place for me. While learning to grow my gifts, I was also gaining courage to look at some of the obstacles that held me back. As spiritual invalids, we would not have survived in a highly charged environment.

It is humbling to consider that God uses broken people to bring His message of hope to others. Barry and I found that the people of Camborne were movingly open to the Spirit. Such is the power of revival that, many years later, the ministries of John Wesley, William Haslam and Billy Bray were still resonant in Cornish hearts. Deposits of hunger for the Spirit were there. They were quick to seize upon crumbs that stirred memories of those great outpourings of power.

Recalling the weekly Friday night gatherings in St Andrew's vicarage, Chorleywood, where we had received the gift of the Holy Spirit, Barry and I were eager to follow that model of meeting to pray. We made it known that people were welcome to join us in prayer on a Friday evening. One young person turned up, followed by a second the following week. This was the prayer powerhouse for St Martin's! Humble and small, it ignited a flame. Others later joined us.

Soon after our move to Cornwall, we had an unexpected visit from an old friend and enigmatic prophet, who dropped in en route to Falmouth to visit his daughter at art college. He was clutching a brown paper carrier bag, which he deposited on the kitchen table with the words, 'That is all that you will need.' He then turned tail and retreated to the front door and vanished. Curious to unpack the contents of the bag, we discovered five bread rolls and two tins of sardines! Clearly this was a message for us to take from the account of the feeding of the 5,000. Jesus took what was available, five loaves and two fish: He gave thanks for the offering and broke it, handing it out to the gathered crowd. There was plenty for everyone and even an abundance of bread left over to gather into baskets (see Mark 6:34-44). It was a challenge to our faith to trust that God would supply for us. We simply had to give what we had, however small. God did take our small offerings and broke them over and over again. The youth club grew, our prayer group grew and we started a home group.

A most unusual group of people assembled for our midweek gathering. One wonderful ninety-two-year-old lady made her way slowly to our house on two walking sticks. She was quite deaf, but loved the fellowship. On one particular evening she, not realising that the Scripture passage was being read, continued a conversation with her friend. Her voice rose above the reading, 'Of course, I can't sleep at night. It's the cats making love in the garden!'

Every afternoon Barry chugged out in our small car to visit parishioners. He worked his way round the houses in the area, introducing himself and asking the householders if they would like him to pray for them. He was usually invited in. It was common practice for regular pastoral visits to be made by the clergy. Barry, once seated, would ask if they had a Bible. It was not unusual for a huge family Bible, covered in dust, to be hauled out of a cupboard for the reading. I relished the stories of these visits when he returned. On one occasion he was asked to join an elderly husband and wife on their sagging sofa to sing a rendition of an old chorus completely unknown to Barry. He manfully made his contribution. I'm sure it would have been memorable for them. It certainly was for Barry.

Cornwall and its people captured our hearts. It remains our favourite place to holiday. Two of our children were born there and are proud to call themselves Cornish. We have so many happy memories of visits to the beach after a storm to gather driftwood that we would dry out to burn in the sitting room fireplace. There it would crackle and spit, giving off blue and yellow flames and a fragrance of the sea that reminded me of shipwrecks and smugglers ferrying contraband through rough seas to rocky coves. In spring, swathes of wild flowers, in pastel hues, draped clifftops and dry stone walls. Local people, reflecting warm and loving hearts, would bring us gifts of vegetables from their allotments, depositing them on our doorstep. We made lasting friendships. Saying goodbye was painful. Our links to the county and the people were strong, drawing us back year after year to a unique place of healing and restoration.

I later had a dream that revealed the transformation that was being worked through the Spirit's healing power. In the dream I found myself in a town marked by beautiful buildings. They were all painted in yellows, blues and terracotta that blended together, making the streets vibrant and interesting. I explored them with wonder. As I studied the architecture I realised that the town was familiar. It was in fact Camborne, where we had been living. God had put these wonderful façades over the grey, worn features, and changed them completely. A voice spoke into my heart: 'You will look back and see what I have done.' .It has proved to be so.

The most precious outcome of my time in Cornwall, as well as the lasting friendships I made, was establishing a regular time of prayer. This has sustained me to this day. Other tables have been my meeting place, but none so precious as that table in a humble Cornish kitchen.

Chapter 3
Forgiveness

When the Lord was busy putting us together, Barry and I learned to minister to each other. We had to look at the darkness, take steps to move into the light and, above all, practise forgiveness. It was the latter that would always bring the final release we needed.

While I was battling with anxiety, Barry was wrestling with bouts of depression. His early years matched mine in terms of insecurity. His parents had divorced when he was very young and, to survive financially, his mother worked while relying on foster carers to look after her son. When she met the man who was later to become her second husband, he made it clear that Barry would not be joining them in the home they planned to set up together. She had to make a choice. Barry was later adopted by the people he came to believe were his parents.

The circumstances of his early beginnings and eventual adoption were relayed to him aged fourteen after a heated row with his adoptive mother. The shock rocked his inner life and cut him off from meaningful communication with his parents for years. He felt betrayed. How could they have withheld this knowledge from him, only to dish it out at a time of teenage instability? He refused to talk about it for years, and only felt able to tell me after our wedding day had been planned. Further discussion about it was discouraged. It was a dark secret festering and threatening to bubble up as we both sought greater intimacy with God.

Depression signalled his past calling for release. Praying together was now our daily practice and gave Barry the confidence to look at the facts about his childhood that he had been unable to face.

Drama is what dominated my early years; not surprising, really, as my parents had met at the Drama Society! Every day at home my mother played out the grief, injustice and frustrations of the unresolved pain of her childhood and the loss of her firstborn child. These emotions were dark and forbidding and they descended on her as each new day began. She struggled to keep them at bay. At the first signs I would run for shelter before they burst out. They affected us all.

Underneath there was a sweetness that rose out of compassion. She wanted to make it right for others who were under such clouds. Small gifts of cakes she had cooked and cartons of seasonal soups were regularly deposited on the doorsteps of ailing neighbours. At home she discharged her own pain and I learned to keep my distance.

In a damaged world, the people who interact with us offer us roles to minimise their own discomfort. I was offered the role of scapegoat. I readily took it on, believing I was responsible for my mother's pain, but believing too that I could make it right. I would strive daily to do this. Of course, I never could. Only the Lord can heal the broken-hearted, but I was too young to see this and daily took up my burden. I bore the guilt of undefined deeds and tried to appease what I was unable to understand.

The great flu epidemic that raged during the First World War took the life of my grandmother, leaving my mother, Lydia, aged four, and her sister, Georgina (known as Ena), aged two, motherless. My grandfather was abroad serving in the army. The sisters were fostered out. My grandfather later married again and two more girls were born. There was a clear division between the half-sisters, and my mother became a reluctant nanny to her younger half-siblings. In later years, meeting my father gave her a happy escape to begin a life for herself.

When Elizabeth Anne was born, followed later by my brother, John, they settled in the New Forest area where my father had been brought up. Their family was complete and life had taken a turn for the better ... only it hadn't. Anne, as she became known, developed meningitis and died. In defence against crippling grief, my mother pushed down the pain. There was little help for the bereaved at the time. She and my father made the decision to have another child as a sort of replacement for the one they had lost. I was born ten months after the death of my sister.

Our uniqueness means that no one can adequately replace another. I certainly did not look the same as Anne. My childhood was already blighted by the shadow of a sibling I had never met.

My mother was frequently irritable and expressed her discomfort by maintaining a silence that blocked me out, sometimes for as long as a week. I came to dread these times. I was laden with the guilt of responsibility. When the pain lifted, the fun-loving, kind person that she basically was emerged again, to my great relief, but the dark episodes left me insecure and cautious. I was fearful of setting up this uncomfortable cycle again. It was wise to tread carefully and to distance myself as much as possible. This pattern went on for years and hindered meaningful communication.

Anne was never mentioned. She was a forbidden subject. When topics came near the danger zone, there was a quick diversion to guide us out. This was quite difficult as weekends were dominated by visits to the graveyard where Anne was buried. The rituals were acted out without mention of the loss. I hated these times. Even now when I think about those Saturdays, I can smell the vase water, soured by decaying flowers, that needed to be emptied before fresh flowers could be arranged and placed on the grave.

Even into her older years, Mum controlled all conversations. She exercised a strange psychological hold over me. I could not break free from it. It made me very angry, especially during my teenage years when the natural pull to independence was countered by the responsibility I was tethered to. Cruel deposits of rage were stirring dangerously within me. It was a relief to leave home to have some respite from it.

Before I left home I had worked locally in a bank. It was a strange choice of occupation for me, totally unsuited to my skills. The boredom of it made me desperate to leave and also to leave home. When typing ledgers one afternoon, an odd idea flitted into my mind. It was really strange. I felt I should pray about a new job and career. I can only imagine that God, a distant figure at the time, was prompting me towards another direction. That evening I knelt beside my bed and did just that, I prayed. Hardly had words left my lips when I clearly heard a voice say, 'You are to train as a nurse.' It did not seem sensational to me; I expected some sort of response, but not that particular career. It was something I had never contemplated before. Within a month I had left the bank, left home and started my nursing training at the Royal Hampshire County Hospital, Winchester. I loved it.

My visits home continued to be uncomfortable and I kept them to a minimum. Meanwhile, my encounter with a group of Christians who hosted a house party I had been invited to attend, while living in Winchester, changed my life irrevocably. Their kindness and sense of fun caused me to ask questions and led me to making a commitment to Christ myself.

Again it was not sensational – my battered emotions could not take too many extremes – but I did feel a shaft of light had entered my inner being, followed by a strange yet undefined unravelling. It was as if a tangled ball of string was unwinding. The inner peace I longed for gained a narrow entrance into my troubled past. I continued to distance myself as much as possible from my family. I did phone from time to time, but there was no guarantee that my mother would be speaking to me.

Incompatible with my Christian life, a growing list of grievances relating to my childhood was being documented within. There were areas that I felt unable to submit to the healing power of Christ. I too pushed them down and avoided situations that probed my insecurities.

God chooses times and places to gently challenge us. It was several years later when I was living in Wick Cottage, Chorleywood, that my challenge to change came. My kitchen, that homely place of food preparation and family gatherings, was the chosen place for the Lord to take me to task. I was preparing coffee for Barry and a friend who had dropped in to see him. A strange and ugly darkness rose up within me, causing waves of guilt and brokenness. I could hardly move. A divine finger was pointing at me. The list that I had rehearsed to convince myself of the validity of the injustice I felt was being held before me. I too was guilty. My hardened attitude, judgements and unkindness were bringing me to account. It was overwhelming. In considerable distress I arrived in the lounge with the tray of coffee and asked for prayer. It was the inner breakthrough leading to a thawing and release that I needed.

Being free of our damaged past is the greatest gift we could receive. Rubbish that clogs up our inner life accumulates over years when it is not faced and cleaned up. When visiting Cornwall now, I love arriving early to stand on the clifftop and view the sandy stretch of beach below, where we had spent the day before. The chaos of hundreds of feet imprinted on the sand, channels dug to create moats around mounds of heaped sand along with the remains of family picnics, have all been swept away in a moment by mountains of surging water powering up the beach, leaving it golden, smooth and unblemished. It is a picture of the cleansing power of forgiveness washing away the inner detritus of years. It is what Jesus offers us through His own life given for us.

We leave footprints of our inner damage throughout our life. I know I have left mine. The giving and receiving of forgiveness washes them away, allowing love to flow again. It can be excruciatingly painful to forgive when we feel justified in holding on to resentment. After His death Jesus reveals Himself to His disciples: 'He breathed on them and said, "Receive the Holy Spirit. If you forgive anyone's sins, their sins are forgiven; if you do not forgive them, they are not forgiven"' (John 20:22-23).

Perhaps He was acknowledging how difficult forgiveness often is, and they, and we, would need the power of the Holy Spirit to release those who have hurt us. In a veiled way it suggests too that we hold the consequences of holding on to grievances. Extending forgiveness is a non-negotiable part of the redemption package. It is a salutary thought. I was glad that I had been brought to account and the beach was at last swept clean.

One of my favourite Bible stories is of a woman who lived on the fringes of society, but found forgiveness and new life through the ministry of Jesus. In Luke's Gospel she is described as having 'lived a sinful life' (Luke 7:37). She came to the house where Jesus was being entertained by one of the Pharisees. Weeping, she wipes Jesus' feet with her tears and pours on them perfume from an alabaster jar. While the Pharisee holds a condemning attitude in his heart, Jesus gently emphasises the grace message He came to bring. We are to forgive. Being forgiven releases huge power to love when our hearts have been clogged up by sin: 'Her many sins have been forgiven – as her great love has shown' (Luke 7:47). This unnamed woman demonstrated what Jesus wants us to know.

Jesus' impending death could not have been far from His thoughts. He knew in detail what it would entail, and prophesied: 'The Son of Man will be delivered over to the chief priests and the teachers of the law. They will condemn him to death and will hand him over to the Gentiles, who will mock him and spit on him, flog him and kill him' (Mark 10:34). Jesus was fully aware of what He would have to face. He confided in His disciples, 'I have a baptism to undergo, and what constraint I am under until it is completed!' (Luke 12:50).

How often did Jesus ask Himself, 'Can I go through with this?' and remember the 'sinful' woman, acting out before Him the power of redemption that His death would release to thousands and thousands? She came with a demonstration of gratitude in an outpouring of love and worship. The perfume rising from her offering mirrored the fragrance that would rise from the sacrifice of His body on the cross. It would reach His heavenly Father, who in response would confirm that it was enough, that the price for sin had been paid.

We all need a scapegoat. Blame goes back as far as Adam. From generation to generation we are shaped by the circumstances and wrong choices made by others. We pass on a varied inheritance of characteristics, strengths, habits and weaknesses. The power that emanates from the past burns deep gullies into our hearts that we are unable to heal without the divine power that is extended to us. I was so glad I had received it. My right to lay blame was taken from me in that moment.

Although there was no immediately obvious change in our relationship, I felt cut free from the rope that had bound me psychologically to my mother. The false guilt I had carried evaporated, making it possible to respond to a true guilt that led me to seek forgiveness.

Inner rages annihilate the goodness in others. But goodness was there in my mother. Later when she had cancer, it rose up. Her vulnerability at that time caused her to seek help from me. It was a new and cherished role. My trips to the south coast were a weekly occurrence and I accompanied her on hospital visits and became her spokesperson for her appointments with the consultant. Mum did not want heroic surgical intervention. It terrified her and would not have been curative. I was able to convey her wishes to the consultant who agreed to relay that choice to the team caring for her. She took to her bed, where she waited for her illness to reach its conclusion.

Distant memories surfaced of a Salvation Army meeting in a hall near where she lived as a young woman. She and Ena found kindness there and they both made faith steps. When Barry asked if she would like him to read a passage of Scripture and pray, she agreed. She found comfort in it. It became our habit when we visited. While she rested, the Spirit was doing a powerful work to bring reconciliation to her troubled past. Although weak, she made meaningful comments to describe the inner changes that were being worked. 'I now know what you mean about the Way,' she volunteered one day. Another time she said, 'Tell Him I want to go.'

For Mum, flowers had been her passion. She planted them in abundance in every available space in the large garden of our family home. In her latter years, when she and my father had moved to a smaller house, she had taken up painting in watercolours. One of the guest bedrooms became her art room, where she would retreat each afternoon to paint; flowers were her chosen subject. (My father painted landscapes in oils in the lounge downstairs. There was an unspoken element of competition between them, which found expression in the wall space they each claimed for their exhibits. My mother's extended from the bedroom, down the stairs to the dining room and beyond, and my father's was a small section of the lounge!)

When Mum was bed-bound I brought fresh flowers, arranging them in a vase that she could see clearly from her bed. I always placed a matching napkin under the vase to enhance the display.

During her final weeks I had a number of vivid dreams. In one of them I was preparing a meal to celebrate my mother's life. On each plate I had placed a different combination of foods with bunches of herbs. I set the table with napkins of deep purple that stood out against the tablecloth. My mother entered the room radiant and happy and came up to me and kissed me on the cheek, something she had never done. Then she said, 'I have never kissed you before. I don't know why.' I believe the herbs were symbolic of a healing of our relationship.

When I visited the following week, I brought flowers in shades of pink and purple and to my amazement I found that the local supermarket had stocked purple napkins. I slipped one under the vase, remembering my dream. Mum was very weak, but managed to say, 'You have always been very good with colour, Mary.' Followed by, 'You are a great comfort to me. I do love you.' They were such healing words for me.

Mum died soon after this. I was invited to see her to say my goodbyes. I really did not want to do this, but I am glad I did. She had died with a smile on her face and looked totally at peace. The Lord had brought a deep reconciliation beyond what I could have imagined. The forgiveness He extended to me, He had also extended to her. Forgiveness is at the heart of the gospel message, won for us on the cross by Jesus, who bore the pain of our human failings. There is no greater power to cut through the shackles binding us to our fallen nature.

I have made coming to this place of power a regular part of my spiritual practice. We cannot shed our humanity with all its shortfalls. We live in a fallen world among bruised people. Their pain rubs off on us and ours on them, but there is a power to heal and restore made available to us through Jesus. It is the most precious of gifts.

Imagining the cross before me in all its starkness has been a visual aid in making this exchange of sin for redemption. I try to do this at least once a week during my morning prayer time. Simply through confession and handing over to Jesus everything that has separated me from Him, and receiving cleansing and forgiveness brings relief and draws me closer in companionship to Him.

Dad later moved to a flat more suited to the needs of his advancing years. To my amusement, the flower paintings of my mother that had dominated the walls of their home vanished, to be replaced by his landscapes. It reflected the healing of the grief he had suffered. He was ready to begin a new life without Mum.

Chapter 4
Herbs and Spices

My favourite kitchen cupboard in my London home is small, measuring 18in x 14in with a depth of 9in. It is made of old pine, has two shelves, is double-hinged and has a brass lever handle. This particular cupboard coaxes me and draws me to open it and rummage and sniff. It is where I keep my herbs and spices, exotic spices on the top shelf and the more familiar garden herbs on the bottom. They jostle with each other when I scrabble to find the one I need, and they often get mixed up.

Barry found the cupboard in an antique shop in Buckinghamshire. I had been expressing frustration with the growing number of small herb jars competing for space in my store cupboard. Hidden behind bags of sugar, pots of chutney, jars of olives and other commodities, they would go missing for months. The cupboard was perfect.

There is something about herbs and spices that represents the essence of all that is good and life-giving. Without them, meals are flavourless, dull and unenticing, yet they can be transformed by a mere teaspoon of one that is complementary to the dish. I like to think that in a Christian community each person, like herbs and spices, brings their own particular flavour to the whole. Everyone has a unique contribution to make.

Following our four years in Cornwall, Barry and I moved to Chorleywood, Hertfordshire, in 1971, firstly under the leadership of John and Gay Perry, and secondly David and Mary Pytches. They were like the 'Herb' and 'Spice' years. John and Gay had transformed the community through their pastoral care. Their ministry brought a flavour of goodness arising from the command to love whatever the cost. It felt good being in Chorleywood, something clearly experienced by others too. I believe this small town was once voted as the most desirable place in England for people to live! Having such role models as John and Gay, who made the ministry of Jesus their constant reference point, was helpful to us. They gave themselves selflessly to helping people get back on their feet, while making them feel that they had a significant role to play in the life of the church. Having had our own personal challenges, Barry and I understood the difficult journey to recovery many parishioners were taking.

Our home, Wick Cottage, was halfway up Quickley Lane and opposite the vicarage. This was good news for our children, Jonathan, Tim and Noonie, because the Perrys had a household full of children of similar ages. A well-worn track was forged between our two houses. Gay and I met up frequently. We both loved the countryside and in season gathered mushrooms and blackberries, always accompanied by children and dogs. It was an added bonus to find an apple tree in full fruit with branches overhanging fences on to the road. We kept a careful eye on one particular apple tree just yards from our homes. Gay was not unknown to rise early in the morning following a storm to fill her basket with the apples that rolled down the hill. I once heard a triumphant shout beneath my bedroom window, 'It's the early bird that catches the worm!' There was Gay with a basket full of beautiful Bramley apples!

Barry had largely been on his own in Cornwall. The rector, who trusted him implicitly to fulfil his role, met him once a week for an hour over a cup of coffee, then again as they gowned up for services in the vestibule before the services. Much of what Barry learned was simply by doing what was expected of a curate – visiting parishioners, running the youth club and preparing sermons. Now, in Chorleywood, we had a wise and highly experienced pastor who sought guidance from the Holy Spirit and acted upon it. It was immensely valuable to Barry to have such a colleague and friend to learn from and test his own vision.

Through their investment in people, John and Gay created a church family at St Andrew's. Everyone was valued, whoever they were. Gay used to say that there was always someone in the congregation who would have a soft spot for even the most unusual members and would befriend them. They knew there was a place for them. It drew comparisons with the psalm extolling the temple as a place where 'Even the sparrow' would find a place in which to have her young (Psalm 84:3). This inclusion of everyone was the strength of the church.

Later when teams were trained to go out to other churches, they were always truly representative of the congregation.

I learned that despite the range of qualities in any group of people there was only one that counted above all others, and that was love: 'Love never fails' (1 Corinthians 13:8). It is the one ingredient that we all need. Whatever else is in the cupboard, that one commodity is needed in every situation relating to humankind. So it was in this climate of love and unwavering dependence on the Holy Spirit that the congregation of St Andrew's grew and grew. This necessitated the building of a new church near the site where the original, known as the 'Tin Tabernacle', had stood.

Vision and growth go hand in hand. Barry, while reflecting on Scripture one day, had an awesome picture of the world as a spinning globe, revealing all the countries of the earth. A harvest field of ripe wheat came into focus, followed by an imprint of words from Acts: 'You will receive power when the Holy Spirit comes on you; and you will be my witnesses in Jerusalem, and in all Judea and Samaria, and to the ends of the earth' (Acts 1:8). Believing this meant that the time had come for outreach to the local area, to places throughout Britain and even the world, he shared his vision with John.

As expected, the Lord had already been speaking to John before Barry's meeting with him. He had been seeking the way ahead for this growing congregation of believers. The Good News of the gospel could not be kept to ourselves. It was time to move out to share it with others. Barry was released from his role as curate to become director of Faith-Sharing. Gradually the vision became clear. Teams under trained leaders would be available to go to churches that extended an invitation. Potential leaders gathered in our home, and the vision was outlined and a training programme decided. I will never forget that first meeting.

Joan Harper, who ran a care home for the elderly, was one of those who came. She stood up and expressed what we all were feeling: 'I feel totally unworthy and ill-equipped to do this, but also excited and humbled to have the privilege of sharing the gospel of Christ in this way.' It broke the ice. We were in this venture together, reliant on the Holy Spirit to help us.

News of the availability of teams gradually leaked beyond the confines of Chorleywood. A slow trickle of invitations came from churches, asking for teams to come to lead outreach weekends for them. The trickle became a flood, and requests came from all parts of the country. Sometimes as many as five or six teams went out to different places.

It was not long before invitations came from further afield also. Because it was difficult for other leaders to get time off work for the extended time required for trips abroad, Barry mostly led those. His travels included trips to India, New Zealand, Africa, Holland, France, Italy, Denmark, Finland, Germany, Sweden, Norway and Russia. Ian Roberts, a retired neurosurgeon, often accompanied Barry and shared the speaking. He and his wife, Joan, were our neighbours. Our two gardens backed on to each other. Joan and I had a signal that we sometimes used to convey a greeting. We could see the silhouetted shapes of each other in the kitchen in the morning and by flashing the kitchen lights made distant communication. There were many of these flashes on Christmas morning when our families gathered to celebrate.

One Christmas Eve, unknown to Joan and Ian, their large fluffy cat, Periwig, climbed through our next-door neighbour's window during the night and feasted on the turkey that was sitting in its oven tray on the kitchen table, ready for roasting! The culprit was not identified for several days and our neighbours generously decided to keep quiet about it when they did find out it was Periwig.

Reports back from Faith-Sharing teams invigorated the church and broadened our horizons. Lasting friendships were forged between team members and people they stayed with in distant parishes. Many of these new friends came to visit St Andrew's. This gave rise to the idea of an 'At Home' weekend. No limit was set on numbers, and dozens of people came. Chorleywood people were amazingly hospitable and accommodation was found for everyone. Later, when the New Wine summer conference was launched, many of the people who had been visited by teams booked to come.

It was hard to believe that a small Hertfordshire town could become the centre of global outreach. Only the Lord could do this. He continues to confound me with His plans and His choices. It is beyond human comprehension. I have always puzzled about Jesus' choice of a young untamed colt to proclaim His kingship in the streets of Jerusalem. There were hundreds of well-worn donkeys that carried people reliably through those ancient passageways, yet He chose to ride a young animal alongside its mother, one that had never worn a saddle, to confront the frenzied crowds shouting, 'Hosanna', and waving their palm branches. Jesus, knowing that questions might be asked about His choice, said, 'If anyone asks you, "Why are you doing this?" say, "The Lord needs it and will send it back here shortly"' (Mark 11:3).

Jesus, by choosing to be without a permanent home, possessions and a regular income, also made a choice to cast Himself on the mercy of others to provide what He needed. Being uncluttered gave Him the freedom to be totally obedient to the promptings of His Father. He trusted Him implicitly. He coaxes us also to make choices to trust Him above our natural reliance on earthly things. This trust is put to the test when unexpected events strip away what we have unconsciously come to lean on. Ill-health, the death of a loved one, the loss of a job, family or friends moving away, fire and flood, all shock us into accepting kindnesses from others. It also directs our prayers to seeking the Lord to provide what we need emotionally and materially to survive. A responsive church community picks up the promptings and moves into action. But most perplexing for those who are the recipients of God's generosity is the unexpected channels through which help often comes.

The Lord works unpredictably. He reminds us that He is God; He does not act as we do (see Numbers 23:19). A small church in Hertfordshire that began as little more than a tin hut would surely not have been the predicted choice to spread the gospel globally.

John and Gay moved from Chorleywood to North Devon, where John took up the post of warden of Lee Abbey. It was sad to see them go. Their farewell could have been likened to that of Paul saying goodbye to the churches as he headed for Rome! Their absence was felt. However, unbeknown to us a spice trail was being forged from Chile to Chorleywood.

David and Mary and their four daughters burst upon the community to stretch our sights beyond this small town with its wooded common, to the hotter, dustier climes of South America. Tales of David riding a horse that he was not quite able to bring under his control, of family life forged in a converted church hall in Santiago, and the exotic strings of the harp bringing music from *Los Paraguayos* brought colour to our gentle pastures.

David was courageous in his pursuit of the Spirit. He and Mary had set out for the mission field a second time, following a furlough spent in England, and Mary knew that, unless the Holy Spirit gave her resources beyond her own, she would not be able to weather it again. Crying out to the Lord on the ship crossing to South America, she was filled with the Holy Spirit who transformed her expectation to one of hope. David, observing this transformation, began his own journey of discovery.

David and Barry became good friends, meeting often and trading off each other's sense of humour. In church there was much hilarity as they, without inhibition, drew attention to the ridiculous in one another. The congregation loved it. When on stage at the New Wine conferences, they sparked off each other in the same way. I believe that in the releasing of laughter many were freed to respond to what the Holy Spirit was doing in the meetings. Those years were characterised by a sense of fun. On a deeper level, the Holy Spirit was bringing transformation to people both at St Andrew's Church and in the conferences.

There was a sense of anticipation within the church whenever we met together. People travelling from miles around queued across the car park to get in. Matt Redman, ever sensitive, often led the worship, bringing us seemingly to the doorway of heaven, where words failed and silence followed. At times it seemed that the very air was charged with supernatural power. During testimony times, people shared stories of their life-changing encounters with God. Dormant gifts of the Spirit, highlighted in Acts, were activated again, and prophecies were given. Occasionally I also had a word to give. I would feel it like a weight in the centre of my being that I could not escape from. It would get heavier and heavier until it was released like an unfolding scroll. Having been discharged, it left me shaken.

Being in church was the highlight of my week. For the first time I understood the essence of King David's words, 'I rejoiced with those who said to me, "Let us go to the house of the LORD"' (Psalm 122:1).

Each weekday morning, from 7 to 7.45am, David ran a prayer meeting in the church lounge. The first quarter of an hour was given to reading a passage of Scripture, followed by brief discussion on what we felt the Lord was saying to us through it. Then we prayed. I loved those mornings and attended as many as possible. I later had the privilege of leading the meetings myself, keeping roughly to the same format. George, who lived locally, came most mornings. He rose even earlier to spend time in prayer at home. By the time he arrived at the meetings, he was so full of what the Lord had been saying to him that we were all caught up in the joy he was so obviously experiencing. It carried us through the day.

I also started a Thursday evening prayer and praise time. It always began with a time of worship. Finding worship leaders was not always easy. Those who led on Sundays and other gatherings could not be expected to turn out yet again for this smaller gathering in the chapel. I was solely concerned that whoever led us would be anointed by the Spirit to lead us into God's presence. Their ability to play the guitar was not high up among my priorities. I often said, 'I would rather that someone anointed by the Spirit strum on a few elastic bands wound round a book, than have a gifted musician who is wooden.' One young student from London Bible College faithfully turned up. He led us wonderfully with the few chords he had mastered. Later Yvonne, a young woman with five small children, came to lead. In rare quiet moments at home she would pick up her guitar and worship. She wrote some beautiful songs that she shared with us on those Thursday evenings. Her songs unveiled her worshipping heart, and brought us powerfully into God's presence. Prayer flowed from such times.

I believe the Lord was constantly drawing us as a church to rely on Him for everything. No meeting would start without prayer. People were released to give words or pictures that would direct us. Worship was always a priority. Years later, when the momentum of that wave of

Holy Spirit power had seemingly run its course, I found myself weeping for the loss of something that was so precious and life-giving.

Chapter 5
Return to Nursing

As our children got older and more independent, I felt the pull to return to nursing. A 'Nurse Bank' had been set up at Mount Vernon Hospital, allowing a flexible system of working for those who had a few hours to spare. I started by working for just three hours a week. It was terrifying! Once I had reported for duty I was sent wherever I was most needed, in any department of the hospital. This meant I ended up in the most fraught situations, on the burns and plastics unit, surgical emergency areas and heart disease wards, where people were battling for their lives. I had quite forgotten the medical jargon that had been so familiar to me in the past. I had to repeatedly ask fellow nurses what they were talking about. Equipment too had been updated, the tubes and dials a total mystery to me. In the car heading for the hospital, I would pray urgently for God's help until I arrived at the gates.

Gradually, like a fog lifting, this mysterious world I had re-engaged with came into clear focus, but this type of nursing was not for me. I felt drawn to cancer care. A new six-week course entitled 'The Dying Patient and the

Family' was beginning at Michael Sobell House, a hospice in the grounds of Mount Vernon. I applied to do it and was given a place. The course covered many of the areas I was interested in, including pain and symptom control and support for the bereaved.

It was a wonderful course and to my surprise, at the completion of the six weeks, I was offered a place working part-time at Michael Sobell House. Even more surprisingly, I was later invited to consider taking on the running of the course. In order to prepare me for this new role, the hospital had agreed to pay for me to do a year's training at Uxbridge Technical College, enrolling in the Teaching in Higher Education course. I ran four or five courses each year and students came from all over the country, many in preparation to become Macmillan nurses. I learned a great deal from those who came. Many were much more experienced than I, and had been working in areas of care for many years, both in hospitals and on the community.

It was a wonderful job. I loved the holistic approach favoured by the unit and made lasting friends of work colleagues who had developed their expertise in the care of patients and their families. There was a huge pool of knowledge to draw from. What I learned was also helpful in the parish, where illness and death were frequent visitors in our tight-knit community. I was able to visit the ill and sometimes borrow equipment from the unit to help them be looked after at home. I often spent time with the bereaved.

A new education block had been erected in the grounds of Michael Sobell House. I had my office there next to those of the Macmillan nurses. The walls were so thin we could communicate without leaving our desks! There was a large lecture room and adjoining library nearby, where courses were run. Every student had allocated times on the unit and out in the community in between lectures.

Each morning I always visited the patients on the unit. One morning I noticed a young woman curled up on her bed, looking out of the window. I went to sit with her. She was clearly in deep sorrow as she faced up to the prospect of saying goodbye to her husband and two young daughters. I asked if she had a pastor to talk to. She responded, 'No, but the lady opposite has regular visits from her vicar, and I strain to hear what he has to say.' It moved me greatly. How could help be given to prepare the dying for such painful separation? Did they know there was a Saviour to help them? Proselytising was frowned upon, but there were opportunities and I took them when possible.

One summer morning, a Jewish man, wearing his dressing gown, was standing in the garden as I arrived for work. He asked if we could talk. He was a medical man at the top of his field. All that he had worked for was coming to an abrupt end with his advancing illness. Sensing his sadness I drew from the writings of the most famous Jewish king, David, who wrote: 'I keep my eyes always on the LORD. With him at my right hand, I shall not be shaken' (Psalm 16:8).

We talked about what that meant in times of trouble. 'Thank you, thank you so much. What you have said is so helpful to me. Can we speak again?' my Jewish friend replied. In fact, there was no other opportunity. He went downhill rapidly that day and died. I was glad I had had a chance to speak to him that morning.

Because we had an open visiting policy, it meant that relatives and friends of the ill were often with their loved ones for long and exhausting periods of time. Once a month I hosted an afternoon tea for them, with some sort of musical entertainment. It gave short respite and diversion from the emotionally exhausting vigil they were keeping. Friends from the church were wonderful in giving their time to help. There were many talented singers and musicians I could call on. My own son Jonathan came to play and sing one afternoon. I was so proud of him. He also gave time as a volunteer, serving tea and coffee to patients and their families, one evening a week.

The unit had a huge volunteer force giving a few hours of their time to serve tea, garden, drive patients to appointments, arrange flowers and even look after the fish tank. This released the trained staff to give more time to their patients.

Because my contract was to work part-time, I was able to work flexibly. This worked well for the holidays, when the children were home, especially if Barry was away with a team. Having started work at the hospital for three hours a week to test whether this was right for me at that time, I ended up working at the hospital three days a week for fifteen years! During this time, Michael Sobell House, in keeping with the gradual evolvement of care for the terminally ill, became known as a centre of palliative care.

The call of God to nurse had reached me in my late teenage years when working in the bank, when in desperation I had prayed for guidance. It led me to pursue a fulfilling career with particular focus on care for the dying and support for the bereaved. It is often said that what we do in the present is a preparation for what lies ahead in the future. God weaves His plan for our lives as we place our trust in Him. I was beginning to feel that a new chapter was opening, but the direction was not clear. I read, 'Enlarge the place of your tent, stretch your tent curtains wide, do not hold back; lengthen your cords, strengthen your stakes' (Isaiah 54:2). Was it time to leave? I wanted this to be confirmed, and looked to the time Barry and I were going to spend at the annual summer conference, hosted by St Andrew's, to give me the answer I needed.

The conference had been started seven years previously and named 'New Wine '89'. It caused some amusement at the beginning when cars pulled into the Bath showground for what they thought was a wine-tasting event, having seen the banners advertising 'New Wine'.

New wine in the Scriptures is a symbol of blessing and God's provision. Vines that had been carefully tended throughout the year were stripped to fill baskets with large juicy bunches of grapes for wine-making. It was a joyful time of thanksgiving. The new had come and wineskins were prepared to contain it. Transitioning to this season was a cause of tension for those who looked back to the old wine as being better. Both old and new would not mix well in the same wineskins. They were incompatible: 'No one pours new wine into old wineskins. Otherwise, the new wine will burst the skins; the wine will run out and the wineskins will be ruined. No, new wine must be poured into new wineskins. And no one after drinking old wine wants the new for they say, "The old is better"' (Luke 5:37-39). The tussle between the old and new, between law and grace, continues. They do not sit well together.

New wine bubbles from a heavenly casket. It is uncontrollable and uncontainable. The conferences were a celebration of a fresh move of the Spirit. There were some surprising manifestations of power in the meetings. The teachings we received put them in a context we could understand.

Over the years a growing number of churches, with their leaders, brought groups from their congregations to the New Wine conference. I always looked forward to these times to renew friendships with people I had not seen for a long time. John and Annie Hughes were old friends and part of the ministry team. Annie asked if we could meet up at the end of one of the morning sessions to pray for each other. She, like me, wanted guidance about the future. After the ministry time we met up. As we started to pray for each other, I had a prophetic word and fell backwards. It was most strange and urgent, and in its message strongly confirmed my thought that I should hand in my notice at Michael Sobell House!

Barry and I left the conference at the end of the week and travelled to Cornwall to stay in a chalet belonging to our friends Alan and Sue, who kindly released it to us for a week each summer. It had been an annual retreat for us, as a family, for years. Our children had now left home. This year the only family member accompanying us was our spaniel, Sophie.

Foremost in my mind was the question of what I would do if, after many years, I no longer made my way to Northwood to work at the hospital. I had a few inflated ideas! Because of my working hours I had been denied the opportunity of travelling to many of the countries Barry had visited to speak at conferences. I warmed to the idea of sharing a stage with him. How wrong could I be?

Throughout the week Barry and I prayed about our future and, despite my vain imaginings, we put our future in God's hands, and covenanted with Him to do whatever He called us to do. Barry was also seeking the way ahead. We had enjoyed wonderful years at Chorleywood, but there was a sense that our time there was coming to an end. David was soon to retire and Barry had agreed to fill the gap during the interregnum, before a new appointment was made.

Together we walked the cliffs overlooking Hayle beach, advertised in holiday brochures as having three miles of golden sands, and prayed. The salty air was invigorating, the sea an ever-changing picture of restless waves rising, only to crash and fall and rise again. God's power was indisputable in this mesmerising display of colour and movement. We felt it. Each day moved us nearer to what felt like a landmark moment, but we had no clear guidance about what we would be doing.

On our last morning while packing up to leave, Barry called me to come outside. Stretched across the Hayle estuary was a perfect rainbow, each strand forming the arc, intense in colour. We knew it was a sign. We had covenanted with the Lord to do anything He asked. He was responding to confirm His covenant with us in a way that believers had understood for generations: 'And God said, "This is the sign of the covenant I am making between me and you and every living creature with you, a covenant for all generations to come: I have set my rainbow in the clouds, and it will be a sign of the covenant between me and the earth. Whenever I bring clouds over the earth and the rainbow appears in the clouds, I will remember my covenant between me and you and all living creatures of every kind"' (Genesis 9:12-15).

We returned home to await clarification of what was as yet unknown. We did not have long to wait.

A few days later in the evening we had a call from Will, our youth leader, asking us to pray urgently. A young person who had attended the youth club some years before, and had kept in touch, had phoned him. He and his family lived in a neighbouring town and no longer came to St Andrew's. A catastrophic situation had arisen at his family home. His mother was injured and the police had arrived. The extent of the problem was not clear, but Will agreed to go to see if he could help. He promised to let us know what was happening. We prayed and waited.

A few hours later another call came through. Tragic news of the death of the mother was relayed, and the arrest of the children's father, who had apparently been responsible. Will stayed on as police, social workers and neighbours all milled round. The children were in shock and had to give their account of events again and again. They were exhausted.

In the early hours of the morning, Will phoned to say he was bringing the children back to Chorleywood. They needed somewhere to go while the forensic team continued to gather evidence. A neighbour had taken them in temporarily. We agreed that they should come to us. We had a lot more space than Will and his new wife, Caroline, who were living in a small one-bedroom flat above the church.

Dylan, Natasha, Bruce and Bianca, young people aged twelve to twenty years, were facing a future with multiple losses. They came to us for breakfast – and stayed.

Chapter 6
The Muffins

It is impossible to measure the breadth of losses experienced by a family for whom circumstances changed irrevocably in a moment. Life, as they had known it, would never be recovered. All we could do was to shore up their defences by providing warmth and security, and an assurance that today they could stay. It was impossible to think beyond the day, or give future reassurances. The first priority was breakfast. They were starving. A 'full English' was what they needed to put some strength back in to them.

Social Services, ever anxious, arrived to view the situation, by which time I had made up beds and informed them that the children would be staying. It was too early to make any firm commitments, but I knew that to separate them would cause further losses. That first day was a blur for all of us. Will and Caroline were the common link between us, and they came to spend time and allow the children to talk. Time drifted by with more official visitors calling to check things out. The police wanted more statements. Supper and sleep brought a welcome conclusion to the day for us all.

I rose early the following morning. Armed with my Bible, I found my prayer place at the kitchen table and opened my Bible to read: 'He gives strength to the weary and increases the power of the weak. Even youths grow tired and weary, and young men stumble and fall; but those who hope in the LORD will renew their strength. They will soar on wings like eagles; they will run and not grow weary, they will walk and not be faint' (Isaiah 40:29-31).

I read it over and over again.

Never had the truth of God's Word been so eagerly taken to heart. I prayed through every phrase, claiming them for myself. Strength for this day was all I sought. I would come again tomorrow to claim the same, and this I did for weeks. God, unveiling the truth of the remarkable exodus of the Israelites from Egypt, tells Moses, 'I carried you on eagles' wings and brought you to myself' (Exodus 19:4). Words painting a wonderful picture of a whole nation being transported on the back of a gigantic eagle, from a life of slavery to a place of safety prepared for them … I felt those wings lifting me up, filling me with strength for another day of unknown challenges.

Our earthly perspective is unable to grasp the unseen world of the kingdom of God that is an ever-present reality. Writers of Scripture, inspired by the Spirit, have given us objects that are familiar to us to help us understand what we do not see physically. The eagle is one of them. Powerful wings that can carry and sweep us away to safety give understanding of the immense power of God to rescue. Rocks that can withstand wave upon wave of water, rising to pound relentlessly upon them, are analogies for God's immovable strength that never gives way. We need to hear these truths to sustain us in testing times. 'Mightier than the thunder of the great waters, mightier than the breakers of the sea – the LORD on high is mighty' (Psalm 93:4).

Each evening before our meal, scriptures that I had written and prepared in advance were pulled out of a small red box. We took it in turns to read them, before praying together. Later, when all the children had left home, I continued to text a daily verse to them. Others asked me to send those same verses, bringing a small ministry to birth. Now those verses are sent to many people both here and abroad. Those who receive them are asked to consider sending them on to others. I love hearing that people have found those verses helpful to them at specific times in their lives when guidance was needed. I even had a report back from Malawi, that BIB (the name of the ministry, echoing the sound of the text arriving and also short for Bible) brought great encouragement to a mission team there, during a time of testing. Our short prayer time around the table became part of our daily routine. Routines were what were needed to give structure and provide security for this battered family. When the children first came we talked together over breakfast to outline how we thought each day might unfold. The first priority at the beginning of their stay was to kit each one out with clothes. Because they had to leave the house abruptly, all they possessed was in their cordoned-off home, and unobtainable. We were told that it could take days before they would be able to get back in to claim their belongings. I said I would take each of the children separately to a large shopping centre. I wanted them to choose what they would like.

Remembering the laboured process of choosing clothes with Noonie, I was not looking forward to this task. Visions of dozens of single shoes scattered over the shop floor as they were rejected, and being returned to boxes by sales assistants, gritting their teeth in suppressed irritation, came before my eyes. I rebuked myself and prayed. The Lord would have to guide if we were to complete this venture.

It was quite miraculous! I prayed with each as we journeyed in the car. With list in hand, we went to their favourite shops, and clothes seemed to fly off rails. They found what they wanted in moments. Praying with them before these trips became a regular part of the shopping routine in months to come.

Day followed day and we still felt unable to discuss the long-term future. It was too early. Barry and I were not yet ready to make a definite decision that would secure their future with us. We needed to be sure that it was right for us, and also for our own family. Social Services continued to be regular visitors. They vaguely mentioned the difficulty they would have in placing the whole family in one home. People came and went. They were part of the support team. They were all very pleasant, drank their tea and coffee, munched biscuits, wrote notes and took their leave.

Food is of huge importance in every household. I had just got used to the reduced numbers in ours. Now we had grown from two to six! The food shopping and cooking of meals took a large chunk of the day. I had received a card from a friend with a tray of muffins displayed on the front. It made me laugh and unconsciously I found myself referring to the children as the Muffins. It was a name that stuck. We were given extraordinary help from the church community, who covenanted to cook on certain days. David and Sue Trevor were wonderful. They lived a few hundred yards from us, had a big house, lots of children and big hearts. Every Tuesday the Muffins went to their home after school for a delicious meal, recounted in detail to me by Bruce, who had and continues to have an affectionate relationship with food. After supper they would spend the evening with the family. They loved those evenings above all others. Tuesday had always been our day off, and being able to continue to have one day to ourselves enabled us to catch our breath, talk out the previous day's events and try to come to terms with our changed situation.

The days drifted by, and Dylan was ready to take up his place at university. He was not sure that he should go. He had taken a huge amount of responsibility for the younger children, and was almost like a father to them. We knew this could not continue. He needed to get a life for himself. Natasha was due to start an art foundation course, not far from our home, that she and her mother had discussed together. She was a very gifted artist. Being able to paint helped her to express the depth of her pain in a way that words could not. Bruce returned to his school nearby. They were kind, but singling him out for kindness made him feel uncomfortable. He wanted to deal quietly with his grief and the many adjustments that were taking place. We managed to get a place in a local school for Bianca (known as B). Like other schools she had attended, it was not an enjoyable experience for her, and we had some interesting times coaxing her to do her homework. At night she suffered terrible flashbacks to the night of her mother's death. I was up night after night with her. I informed the school that it would not be reasonable for her to attend when she had had so little sleep. Instead we went for long walks on the common with the dog. She talked and talked, trying to make sense of years of dysfunction in the family home.

My growing conviction was that the Muffins should stay with us on a permanent basis. We were both becoming increasingly fond of them and I was reluctant to consider them being placed with another family. Drifting into my consciousness was my commitment to do whatever the Lord wanted me to do. This was surely it! I put my case to Barry. He was still unsure.

Notice came that the Muffins could now have a funeral service for their mother. We had a moving service of thanksgiving at St Andrew's, which Barry took. The Muffins all gave tributes. It was a final goodbye, and the Lord used this moment to speak to Barry, confirming that He had given this family to us to love and to parent. Our own children were incredibly generous in their response, opening their hearts to their new siblings, knowing that life for them too would also change.

Grief is expressed individually, according to the personality and the depth of the relationship the bereaved person had with the dead person. It was different for each of the Muffins. Natasha had been closest to her mother and grieved painfully. At times she was incapacitated, unable to go to college and wanting to just curl up in bed. It was clear that professional help was needed. A psychiatrist specialising in loss suffered by children of murdered parents was recommended. We went up to his London clinic weekly. It gave them all a chance to articulate the deep feelings that swirled around uninvited and would later break out in unguarded moments. It helped them to manage their grief while having a safe outlet where what they were experiencing was understood.

B had begged me to allow Sophie to have puppies. In a weak moment I agreed and found a handsome local golden cocker spaniel whose owner was keen to make some money from his services. B gave a detailed report of the liaison between the two dogs to her siblings! Four beautiful puppies were born in the kitchen of Wick Cottage, one each for the Muffins to hold in the evenings.

Looking back, we had some amusing moments setting in place workable practices within the home. The Muffins had a good sense of humour and we worked with that as much as we could. Friday was the day for meeting up with friends after school and college. I named it 'Tidy Friday', and encouraged them to clear up the chaos in their bedrooms before going out. Then there was the cooking. Meals at their home were mostly pre-packed ones from the supermarket. I thought it would be a good idea if they learned to cook. They took it in turns to do this on Thursdays, using a cookery manual with step-by-step instructions to help them through the basics, with often interesting but surprisingly good results.

I knew it would be impossible for us to recreate family life as the children had known it, and made clear that, however difficult, the Muffins would have to make the adjustments to us. It made sense that we all agreed that they were a welcome part of our family and needed to be fully integrated, but of course it also meant more changes for them. I did try to comply with things that were especially important to them. Christmas was important to B. Their family had celebrated extravagantly and their mother had recently bought new beautiful decorations, not like ours. B's look of disdain confirmed that I would have to up my game! I bought new ones that met with her approval.

Reports were coming back from the Muffins' father that he was extremely unhappy with their accommodation with a Christian family. He attributed the tensions at home to his wife's Christian faith. The children being housed with a pastor was the worst-case scenario for him. Social workers remonstrated with him and told him that the children were happily settled, but his anger was unabated. The children themselves were still trying to come to terms with the violence that had shaken their family life and were not yet ready to visit their father. This compounded his anger, which was relayed to us through phone calls from his older brother. Menacing darkness threatened us whenever these phone calls were made.

Even before the calls came, I could feel turbulence in my soul. Barry took the calls and I would pray urgently. Powers of darkness are as much a reality as the powers of light. They are not confined by space and reach their target even across the airwaves. There were many battles for us to fight in those early months. Sadly, news came the following year that the children's father had taken his own life. It left them orphaned and with yet more deep pain to work through. They had not seen their father since the fateful night of the death of their mother.

Grief takes its own course and cannot be conveniently dismissed. Sometimes it will reassert itself years after the loss. It was definitely at its most intense in the first six months, and then again about a year later, when the full implications of multiple losses began to be unpacked. In between these times, friends from the church felt it would be good for Barry and me to have a break. They would pay for us to go to New Zealand for three weeks. It was an exciting prospect.

Richard and Ingrid, friends from the church and Faith-Sharing team leaders, volunteered to move into Wick Cottage to look after the Muffins, and Sophie, whose puppies by this time had been happily settled in new homes. Richard and Ingrid had already given up a whole summer a couple of years before to act as house parents to the relays of teams covering the teaching programme at a Bible school in Siberia. They were clearly generous with their time, as well as being adventurers. Their stay at Wick Cottage proved to be a greater adventure than we or they had anticipated!

When God covenants with His people, those agreements stand firm forever. We recalled the week in Cornwall when we promised to do anything God asked us to do. The sign of the rainbow sealed that covenant for whatever lay ahead. Our faith in God had not been misplaced.

Twenty years later we were able to celebrate the two decades that had passed since the arrival of the Muffins at our home in Chorleywood. Now they were all married with children of their own, we gathered near Richmond for coffee, followed by a picnic on the banks of the Thames that they had organised. As we sat on rugs drinking champagne from plastic cups and the grandchildren paddled in the Thames, licking their ice lollies, we recalled with mirth the many ridiculous moments we all had adjusting to each other. We had a wonderful time together and Barry and I were greatly moved by the cards they had written for us.

Psalm 23, above all the psalms written, expresses the tender relationship between God and His people. Trusting in Him as the Good Shepherd ensures the very best outcome for us, His sheep. There is no covering over of the difficulties that are part of our life's journey. We will have them. Human weakness as expressed in tiredness, hunger and lack of inner resources will repeatedly thwart our endeavours. The Lord knows this. In the darkest of times, when it seems that the shadow of death itself pursues us, we can be confident that He will bring us through to victory. Only He can do this. Shadows attach themselves to our feet and cannot be shaken off. They relentlessly follow us, but the Lord can change that destiny of darkness. He cuts off the shadows and replaces them with His goodness and mercy – they are what follow us all our earthly life when we place our trust in Him.

People have kindly commended us for opening our home to the Muffins. It would be wrong of us to take their praise. Only God has made possible this unexpected venture and it is to Him that we bow in thanksgiving.

Chapter 7
Trip to New Zealand

The warning signs were there the moment the plane touched down at Auckland Airport in January 1997. Torrential rain was sweeping across the tarmac as we fought our way to the terminal building. Cyclones had already hit the north of the island earlier in the month, and the unseasonably wet and windy January weather had not abated.

Ian McCormack, known widely as 'The Jellyfish Man',[1] met us at Arrivals. Ian and his wife, Jane, had stayed with us in England a number of times when on preaching tours to give his testimony. His life had been turned around dramatically following fatal box jellyfish stings and waking up in a mortuary! Seeing him again, in his native New Zealand, seemed, in retrospect, to be significant, as our visit turned into a memorable sea adventure.

Ian had driven up from Tauranga, on the east coast of New Zealand, to see us, and handed us his car keys. His

---

[1] If you haven't heard Ian's amazing story of life beyond death, read *A Glimpse of Eternity* (CreateSpace, 2014).

new car had been a gift from a friend a few days previously. It was a generous act to lend it to us for our long journey down to Palmerston North, where Barry's mother had recently relocated. We spent a night at Bucklands Beach, Howick, near where Barry's parents had had their family home, before making the trip south. We wanted to make the most of the three weeks ahead.

Time passed quickly, meeting up with family members, taking Barry's mother out and just enjoying exploring the area. Near the end of the third week, we had a much longed-for sunny day. I sat up in bed early and began my usual practice of praying and committing the day to the Lord. I suddenly felt myself transported from my bedroom to a railway embankment covered with grass of an intense green. In the distance I could hear the roar of a steam train powering down the tracks. As it passed by, I heard a voice say, 'Nothing will stop my plans and purposes!' As it vanished into the distance a mocking figure appeared, filling me with apprehension. The vision faded and I was back in the bedroom, feeling extremely puzzled by this strange scenario. I shared it with Barry, who was just surfacing from sleep. He was no clearer than I about the meaning of it. We prayed together and planned to make the most of this rare sunny day to take Barry's mother Dorothy and his sister Jan out for lunch at the Esplanade. If the weather held, we would later go to the beach by ourselves and hopefully have a swim.

The Esplanade, on the main highway to Massey University, is a beautiful place to walk. It has wooded pathways with native trees, open spaces with grassy areas for children to play, fishponds and well-tended flowerbeds, with bright seasonal flowers. A separate area is sectioned off as a huge rose garden, with roses of every colour and kind. It even has an aviary with a variety of native birds, many nearly extinct and only usually seen in the South Island of New Zealand. After exploring the gardens, we made our way to the restaurant for lunch before dropping Barry's mother and Jan back home. It was the best day we had had since our arrival. We grabbed our towels and swimming costumes and headed for Himitangi Beach, a few miles out of the city.

Firm sand allowed cars to drive right up the beach to be close to the best surfing areas. Barry could hardly wait to get into the waves to bodysurf. I found a sheltered spot higher up the beach, sat on my towel and read my book. A chill breeze was coming off the sea and I decided not to swim. It was clear that the weather was about to change. Although not late, the light was fading rapidly and ominous black clouds were forming above the horizon, making the water look menacingly inky. Waves were rising to exciting levels for surfers. It was what they had come for.

Engrossed in my book, I had hardly noticed when many surfers began to call it a day and come in. My attention was abruptly aroused. Two small children were heading in my direction, and calling to me.

'Come quickly! Your husband has been injured.'

My immediate thought was that Barry had cut his foot on glass. I hurried down the beach to find him curled up in pain and being cared for by a large tattooed lady, into whose arms he had fallen as he staggered up the beach.

Between groans he told me he had been dumped by a huge wave that had seemingly come from nowhere. His neck was in agony. I hastily rolled a towel to make a brace to secure it. He would need to get to the hospital. A young man introducing himself as the lifeguard called an ambulance.

Fear gripped the pit of my stomach as we waited on the beach. Most people had already left for their homes. Distant clouds were rolling towards the beach. It was getting darker and darker.

I prayed urgently. 'Lord, I don't know anyone here. Unless You send help there is little I can do.'

Time stood still. Barry was greatly distressed and I could do nothing for him. The wait seemed endless. At last the ambulance made its way up the beach. Barry was rolled on to a stretcher. We were ready to go to the hospital at Palmerston North, about half an hour away.

Out of the gloom the tattooed lady reappeared. She had been anxiously watching from a distance and now stepped forward.

'I'll follow the ambulance in your car so you won't have to worry about leaving it here,' she said.

At the hospital she handed over the keys and vanished before I was able to thank her. God has His servants everywhere. I was about to meet many more.

The houseman on duty at the Accident and Emergency centre greeted us at the entrance. He had Barry transferred to a hospital stretcher. Leaning over him, he said, 'Would you like me to pray with you?' God was with us, the future was unknown, but we knew we would be taken care of.

As suspected, an X-ray confirmed that Barry had broken his neck. Four bones had been fractured. Our hopes of returning to the UK the following week were dashed. He was transferred to a Stryker bed on the orthopaedic ward, given some powerful sedation and settled for the night. A Christian staff nurse who was on duty that evening prayed with us, and reassured me that Barry would have good care. I made my way back to Barry's mother's house. I was exhausted.

My first priority before falling into bed was to get word to our family. They, in turn, promised to circulate the news to our friends and ask them to pray. I phoned Richard and Ingrid, who were expecting to be released from their duties at Wick Cottage in a few days. What would happen to the Muffins?

'We'll stay as long as is needed,' they responded.

God was putting stabilisers in place for each situation of concern. My mind was in overload. I could not think. I had to go back to my practice of living one day at a time. There was nothing more I could do now but sleep.

The next day I packed my bag early and headed for the hospital. A room had been found for me in the doctors' on-call residents' block. This would be my home for the next few weeks. It was agreed that I could work an informal shift, morning and evening, helping with Barry's basic care. Teams of nurses came into his cubicle every few hours to turn him on the Stryker bed. It was a terrible experience for him, being turned 90 degrees to change his position. He said he felt as if his brain was being scrambled and likened the experience to one of a barbecued chicken. Once over, he could look towards the floor through a hole in the bed, designed for this purpose. I was able to position his Bible below for him to read. He wanted to read from the book of Isaiah. While being tossed in the waves, a scripture from that book had powered through his mind like words being spoken directly to him: 'When you pass through the waters, I will be with you; and when you pass through the rivers, they will not sweep over you. When you walk through the fire, you will not be burned; the flames will not set you ablaze' (Isaiah 43:2).

We read it again together.

The following day our son Jonathan sent us a verse: 'Your path led through the sea, your way through the mighty waters, though your footprints were not seen' (Psalm 77:19). God was unfolding a purpose we were yet to fully grasp.

My reliance on routines put a structure into the days. I arrived at ten o'clock each morning and stayed with Barry until lunchtime. I came again in the evening. Being unable to move and having limited outlook, either the floor for a brief period or a square patch of white ceiling, reduced all activities and provided no diversion. Together we devised a programme for each day, which included reading the Bible and praying, followed by 'news from home'.

Each day, post was delivered to us. Cards and fax messages came flooding in, causing great fascination to the ward staff. It blessed us so much to hear from friends and family. James Roberts, who had regularly travelled with Barry and was a close friend of ours, kept the church updated with news and continued to encourage people to write. We had literally hundreds of letters and cards, which were a lifeline in a world that was rapidly vanishing. Occasionally one of our children would get through to the ward phone, which was dragged through corridors on wheels to Barry's room. Hearing their voices again brought great comfort to us. My friend Shirl always seemed to get through at key moments. Having someone who knew me well to talk to helped me offload some of my fears.

Days passed and still no decision regarding future treatment had been made. Then late one afternoon there was a knock on the cubicle door. A young fair-haired man came in.

'You don't know me,' he started. 'I heard you were here and know you have ministered in many parts of New Zealand. I also am a pastor and I minister at the Christian Community Church in Palmerston North.' His name was Nigel Dixon. He then told us that he had had a growing conviction that he should come to visit Barry. On his journey to the hospital, Scripture verses kept coming to him.

'Have you got a Bible?' he asked.

He turned the pages and began to read, 'When you pass through the waters, I will be with you; and when you pass through the rivers, they will not sweep over you. When you walk through the fire, you will not be burned; the flames will not set you ablaze.' It was deeply moving to hear those now-familiar words from Isaiah read yet again, words that God had clearly spoken at Himitangi. Barry would emerge from this. We believed, despite the seriousness of his injury, there was a future of hope ahead.

Nigel continued to visit and introduced us to the senior pastor. The Christian staff nurse we had met earlier often stayed to talk and her daughter, who also worked in the hospital, came up to see us during lunch breaks. Suddenly we had local friends and I started attending the Christian Community Church, and even preached there one Sunday morning! They were all so kind. Our borrowed car from Ian had been collected and the church arrived with another one for me to use!

One afternoon the whole surgical team crowded around Barry's bed. A decision had been made.

'We have good news and bad,' the consultant began. 'In two days' time we are going to operate. This could get you on your feet again or – the worst-case scenario – you could end up paralysed. We have to warn you of this. We cannot keep you indefinitely on this bed. We are going to take you to theatre for an operation and you will be returned here. The operation will take many hours and a neurological surgeon will be joining the orthopaedic team.' News at last, but it had a bite. The words from Isaiah came flooding back.

Nigel came in the night before the operation, and anointed Barry as directed in Scripture: 'Is anyone among you ill? Let them call the elders of the church to pray over them and anoint them with oil in the name of the Lord. And the prayer offered in faith will make the sick person well; the Lord will raise them up' (James 5:14-15).

Back in my room, a long day loomed ahead. Preparation for Barry's operation began early that morning. I was able to see him briefly before the staff swarmed in purposefully, armed with charts, medications and the familiar shapeless, pastel gown worn by patients. It was time for me to leave. I would need to plan my day to keep my mind from straying down roads to anxious thoughts.

I took the road down to the small shopping area to find somewhere to have a cup of coffee. It was good to breathe fresh air. I tried to pray, but my emotions were in lockdown, and it was difficult to focus. Time was dragging. After gazing listlessly in shop windows, I turned back. Opening my Bible, an obscure passage caught my attention. It was from the book of Numbers: 'Gold, silver, bronze, iron, tin, lead and anything else that can withstand fire must be put through the fire, and then it will be clean. But it must also be purified with the water of cleansing '(Numbers 31:22-23).

It strangely seemed to link to the passage from Isaiah 43. Both water and fire seem to be God's instruments to prepare us for service. In the temple, implements for worship were all put through water, but those used for specific tasks were put through fire. There was no escape from water and fire. The message was coming from all directions.

Other words were flooding my mind as the hours passed and there was still no news from the ward, only, 'No, he is not back yet. He is still in theatre.' 'We have good news and bad' was pitted against, 'This could get him on his feet again, but he could end up paralysed.' I harnessed my thoughts by writing out as many words as I could find in the NO SMOKING notice above the door of my room. Seven hours after the scheduled operation time, I took courage in hand and phoned the theatre. Barry was back in the recovery room and 'yes', the operation had been a success! I hurried over to see him.

A week later, Halo traction was fitted. This is a cruel metal structure, secured by nails hammered into the skull, and harnessed by straps to the chest. For the first time in weeks, Barry was able to stand and eventually to walk. He was desperate to escape from the room that had seemingly imprisoned him. It was agreed that we could find a motel near the hospital to stay, with the understanding that we would attend regular appointments at the hospital. Again the church came to our aid. A surgeon and member of the congregation offered to help me explore the area for suitable temporary accommodation. We found a motel; not only was it right opposite the Esplanade, but also had a room with a Jacuzzi that Barry could use. The people who ran the motel were the loveliest people and became good friends.

Both Barry and I found it therapeutic to have a daily walk round the gardens that we had explored on the fateful day of the accident. Life was beginning to normalise, despite the frequent appointments at the hospital. The pastor from the church borrowed a wheelchair and even took Barry to watch a rugby match. Our new Christian friends would often invite us back to their homes for meals. Nigel continued to call and we met his wife, Carolyn.

Barry hated the Halo traction and begged to have it removed. Each week his consultant said, 'We'll see in another week.' It was endless. When news eventually came that it was to be removed, we were jubilant. A less intrusive brace was fitted and news was relayed that we could begin to plan our trip back to England. It was so exciting! Our three-week holiday had morphed into three months. John and Jane helped us to pack, and a taxi was called. As we stood together waiting for our transport, a huge rainbow formed in the sky above us. Our destiny was assured. God was with us.

Chapter 8
Give!

Bread has a powerful quality to draw us to the kitchen. I used to bake bread, dense rustic rolls, described by my brother John as being aggressively healthy. I know what he meant. They were crunchy with grain from a mill in Suffolk that arrived in hessian sacks. To get the right consistency for bread flour, I ground it in an old-fashioned coffee grinder attached to the wall in the kitchen. It was a bit of a chore and I latched on to the crafty plan of getting the children and their friends to compete to see how much they could grind in a defined period of time. Their exertions produced coarse flour that cascaded into a bowl ready for step one of its transformation into puffy brown rolls.

It was a delight to open the oven door and smell the first wave of the nutty, yeasty mounds, uniform in size and sitting side by side in the baking tin like happy siblings. I had forgotten that God too could smell until I reread the book of Exodus. Giving our very best in a spirit of generosity apparently releases a fragrance.

Cornelius, a Roman centurion, was a generous supporter of the Jewish community. He gave money for the upkeep of the synagogue and, as a believer in God, prayed regularly. His actions are described as releasing a fragrance that actually reached the nose of God. I believe He smelt it, loved it and sent an angel who told Cornelius, an uncircumcised Roman soldier, a Gentile, how pleasing this was to God. 'Your prayers and gifts to the poor have come up as a memorial offering before God' (Acts 10:4). Perhaps it reminded Him of a covenant relationship with a nation He had chosen for Himself.

The new covenant God had established with all humankind through the death of Jesus was also confirmed in the coming of the Holy Spirit to this non-Jewish believer.

Systematically wading through the books of the Bible, I was struck by the many passages related to giving. I began recording them in a notebook. They challenged me. Apart from the annual talk in church that called upon my purse, I had not taken this aspect of my Christian faith seriously. I did try to put a tenth of my earnings on the collection plate, but I had not yet seen that giving was a way of life that released blessings, setting in motion kingdom principles.

Worldly wisdom is often contrary to the ways of the kingdom of God. In fact, God's ways make little sense at all in the face of accepted logic. It takes huge measures of faith to align one's ways to them. There are strange verses such as 'Anyone who loves their life will lose it, while anyone who hates their life in this world will keep it for eternal life' (John 12:25). These words are in sharp contrast to the drive to be personally fulfilled and go for what you want. Living sacrificially with altruistic goals in order to enrich the lives of others is not a popular way of thinking, yet God makes it clear that He is in favour of this.

One of the strangest accounts of provision is recorded in 1 Kings 17. Here we are introduced to Elijah, an acclaimed prophet in Israel. In a time of drought and ensuing famine, Elijah is fed by ravens. God sent them. Weird in itself! Later, when the famine really kicks in, he is instructed to go to Zarephath where he will be taken care of. Logic would suggest that he would be directed to a wealthy family who had ample provisions, but no, he is told to go to a poor widow. Even stranger, she is down to her last measure of flour and a little oil with which to make a meal for herself and her son. It could not be stretched further. Kingdom ways are put to the test when Elijah, instructed by God, tells her, 'First make a small loaf of bread for me from what you have and bring it to me, and then make something for yourself and your son' (1 Kings 17:13). No other explanation is given until she responds to his request. This releases the provision God intends for her, her son and also Elijah. Elijah speaks the prophetic word given him: 'The jar of flour will not be used up and the jug of oil will not run dry until the day the LORD sends rain on the land' (1 Kings 17:14). Illogical, incomprehensible, these are the ways of God. Whether rich or poor, we all have good reasons to hold on to what we have, but God invites us to enter into the adventure of giving. Can you imagine the joy and the wonder experienced day after day when quite miraculously the flour arrives in the jar and yet again the jug is filled with oil? It was all triggered by that initial step of faith. God's ways are not like ours (see Isaiah 55:8). Because of this we repeatedly have to adjust our perceptions to see when God is at work. He does things differently, bringing His purposes to birth in ways that sometimes seem strange.

Bad experiences of poverty can obstruct our ability to give generously, and hinder these faith adventures that God would involve us in. This happened in my family. My great-grandfather gave each of his four children a house. In a careless gambling venture, my grandfather lost his, reducing his family's assets to nil. My father experienced the extreme hardship of those years and strove to pull his family out of the pall of poverty, as well as dealing with the struggles brought about by the war years. He did well. Buying land, he built us a home and we were well provided for without the humiliation of debt, but it came at a cost. Money was greatly respected in our household. There was an accounting for everything. Money was to be saved or used sensibly. I got the message, that is, until I read scriptures that suggested otherwise. I had work to do. It resulted in having to make radical habit changes.

Changing old attitudes takes perseverance. It is easy to fall back into them again in unguarded moments. To develop the open-handedness that God expected of me, I put into practice some loosening-up exercises. Giving in small ways, to my surprise, in time became addictive. I could not stop. It was hilarious and wonderful. When queueing in the supermarket, I would step in and pay when poorer people, having exhausted their funds, had to

110

hand back goods from their shopping baskets. I scribbled out cheques for people who had come for prayer at church because of debt problems. My attention was drawn to items in shops that I thought friends would appreciate. It was celebratory. God was my provider. He alone gives us all we have. In small ways, I could share it with others. What could be happier? The fact is, we can never outgive God.

Giving is meant to be joyful. Dismal days followed dreary months in Israel when the harvest failed. Crops, starved of rain essential for their full development, just dried up and shrank to the ground. Vines drooped. The plump lush grapes that brought the promise of barrels of rich red wine shrivelled on sagging stems, and olives as small as pips dropped pitifully into the dust. It was disastrous. Joel who records this terrible scene states in chapter 1 of his book that the priests who ministered before the Lord were in mourning. Not only were there empty grain stores and wineskins, but there were no happy celebrations. Thankfulness, joy and the acknowledgement that all good things come from God were at the heart of harvest thanksgiving. Giving and celebration are meant to go hand in hand.

When joy is absent and we give grudgingly, our reluctant giving is etched on our hearts and read by God. My discovery of the joy, addiction and hilarity of giving is one of the most precious discoveries I have made. I still need to remind myself repeatedly of the truths surrounding what has been entrusted to us by God. He expects a good return for His investment.

Post-war Britain was rightfully named 'Austerity Britain'. The 'make do and mend' culture forged through necessity during the war years enabled people to survive with ever-diminishing resources. People were marvellously creative in making their limited means stretch to provide for their families. I was brought up in such a culture and my parents were brilliant at managing what little they had. Like many of their contemporaries, they had a great respect for what was available and an abhorrence of waste. Even when the economy picked up this established way of life continued. Everything was filtered through the questions raised during times of scarcity, 'Can I afford this?', 'Is this a good use of money?' It made us, as 'war years' children, unnecessarily accountable long after the war had ended. The threat of poverty had lifted, yet we continued to live under it. It was difficult to break the habit and to be more open-handed with what we had. It put a brake on the small acts of kindness that bring warmth to relationships.

Fear of poverty and lack of provision test our faith. When the future looms with uncertainty it casts a shadow over us, and fear creeps into our souls. We forget that other principles beyond human understanding are bidding us to take steps of faith beyond reason.

In my imagination I picture rows of costly jars of perfume stored in heaven, each labelled with the name of the giver, bottles that represent sacrificial acts of generosity. God knows them all. At appointed times He responds in kindness to us. In the material world in which we live, money and provision occupy much of our thoughts. Jesus draws a clear line between this world and the unseen world of the kingdom of God. On earth we do have monetary responsibilities; those responsibilities have to be respected, but we have a greater obligation to God our Provider. No particular limit is set on this, although historically the Jews set aside a tenth of their income in response to God's command, 'Be sure to set aside a tenth of all that your fields produce each year' (Deuteronomy 14:22). Wonderfully, the needs of the whole community were met through this system of giving, known as the sacred portion. It was founded on compassion: 'When you have finished setting aside a tenth of all your produce in the third year, the year of the tithe, you shall give it to the Levite, the foreigner, the fatherless and the widow, so that they may eat in your towns and be satisfied. Then say to the LORD your God: "I have removed from my house the sacred portion and have given it to the Levite, the foreigner, the fatherless and the widow, according to all you commanded"' (Deuteronomy 26:12-13).

Giving is directly related to a value system forged in heaven. It evades human understanding. We tap into it when we give generously and warmly. We find that provision flows back to us in unexpected ways that build our faith. Crippling money anxieties are replaced by trust in our Provider. It is exciting to see how He does it. God is preparing us on earth for a culture He has shaped in heaven.

Each day we wake as receivers of the grace God extends to us. We are continually being blessed by His generosity. Perfect gifts are memorable, reflecting we are truly known by the giver. Psalm 139 confirms that God knows us completely. As our heavenly Father He knows how and what to give to His children.

My earliest memory of receiving a gift was for my fourth birthday, when a friend of my mother called with a bunch of flowers gathered from her garden, for me! Not the usual gift to give a child. I loved it. I remember her coming round the path at the side of the house and holding it out to me. The pleasure of that moment remains. It was a perfect gift. It also confirmed that even at that young age I was known.

From the earliest of times, fatherhood is dropped into our concept of this mysterious being we call God. That is how He wants us to relate to Him. Wonderful graphic pictures of His fatherly involvement are described in Scripture: 'You saw how the LORD your God carried you, as a father carries his son … ' (Deuteronomy 1:31), and 'He will not let your foot slip – he who watches over you will not slumber … The LORD will keep you from all harm – he will watch over your life … your coming and going both now and evermore' (Psalm 121:3-8). Faith is kindled when we can trust in God's fatherly care for us. He does not want us to be immobilised by worries concerning provision.

God's voice comes unexpectedly to us in impacting and memorable moments, underlining what we need to know to trust Him. One autumn, I was in North Carolina staying with our friends Alex and Susan McAllister, when the maple trees were ablaze with beautiful colours. I loved walking through the roads near their home that were filled with papery leaves of all shades and finding my way up to the main highway. It was here that God spoke to me, not in a way that one would commonly associate with God. An electronic voice boomed out as I reached the pedestrian crossing, telling me that I was on 'Providence Road'. Not once but three times I was informed, 'Providence Road, Providence Road. You have come to Providence Road.' It could not have been clearer. Providence, one of those words on a gradual slide from common usage, means to be under the kindly hand of God: in other words, His blessing. The word 'provide' also comes from providence. It was reassuring to know I was going to be provided for and God was going to do it.

Having an unshakeable belief that I am indeed on that road protects me from the anxieties that attach themselves to money. It allows me to be thankful, something God expects of me. How much more should we express our thanks?

Financially, things were difficult for us when Barry was serving his first curacy. A curate's salary was one of the lowest. We did not receive expenses to top it up. It took ingenuity to stretch our scant means to heating, running a car, entertaining, general housekeeping and providing for our three children. I was grateful for the skills I had learned at home in earlier days. When in Cornwall I lived in a poor community among people who also had to cope on low incomes. We were in it together. It was a kind community where bags of vegetables from allotments were left on doorsteps, as I mentioned earlier. Our elderly neighbour would often hand me delicious pasties, straight from the oven, over the stone wall that divided our properties. Cornish teas were characterised by abundance. Huge plates of sandwiches and home-cooked cakes and biscuits filled tables covered with freshly laundered cloths. Cups were replenished with tea from large brown teapots. These were happy times and I do not remember money being much mentioned.

Harvest festivals were celebrated annually in Cornwall, not only in churches, but also in other places of meeting. Even the rugby club had a yearly gathering where hymns of thanksgiving were sung and local produce given for distribution to poorer members of the community. Barry played for the local rugby team and when we first moved to Camborne we were invited to join them for their harvest celebration. The person inviting us forgot to mention that the club would like Barry to give a short address. When he was introduced as the guest speaker and called forward to give a word, the shock of the moment propelled him to his feet and he somehow managed to cobble some godly thoughts together.

God opens our eyes to the riches of His provision. Providence Road is a wonderful road to be on. I want to stay on that road, believing that God's hand of blessing is over me. All that I need will be provided. I can give generously, holding on loosely to what I have, knowing that this pleases Him. In return I have the assurance that I am His portion! 'For the LORD'S portion is his people' (Deuteronomy 32:9).

Chapter 9
Move to London

God made it clear to Moses, when he was leading the nation of Israel, that they would not be putting roots down until they had laid claim to the land promised them. This was unsettling. They were just beginning to savour their new freedom, but their trust in God for provision would repeatedly be put to the test. Arriving at Elim, a place of springs and palms, mirroring the pictures featured in the travel brochures posted through our letterboxes in January, must have brought relief and respite from the weariness of their journey. 'Then they came to Elim, where there were twelve springs and seventy palm trees, and they camped there near the water' (Exodus 15:27). It was not to last; it was yet again time to move on. No wonder there was grumbling in the camp! No, they were to be a pilgrim people, and so are we. God is eager to get us to the destinations He has planned and prepared for us, not always where we would choose to be, but always the best.

God does not do 'boring'. He is, after all, 'the author of life' (Acts 3:15). Life is what emanates from Him, and He leads us to where we will find it. God had a wonderful plan for the Israelites, to bring them to a land overflowing with potential for development, with rich crops and grazing pasture for their sheep and cattle, where each family could build a home for themselves. To capture their imagination further He had described it as 'a land flowing with milk and honey' (Exodus 3:8): a bit sticky, but they knew what He was saying. This land would be the best.

The Lord commanded Moses to send out leaders from the tribes to explore it before they made the final crossing as a nation. Their report would confirm everything that was promised. An enormous bunch of grapes carried between two poles was evidence. This was the account of the explorers: 'We went into the land to which you sent us, and it does flow with milk and honey! Here is its fruit' (Numbers 13:27). Giving them just enough time to marvel at this amazing news, the explorers took a breath and said, in the next verse, 'But ... ' What followed swept away the Israelites' dreams, put fear in their hearts and rooted them in the wilderness for years. There would be opposition. What's new! Fear entered and everything that they had hoped for came to nothing. Forty dreary years followed. Yet another circuit of the wilderness filled their days, another predictable meal of quail.

God has good plans for us too. We had been resident in Chorleywood for nearly thirty years and it was clear we needed a new challenge. It had been four years since the Muffins came to us. David had retired and Barry was working under the leadership of a new incumbent. He knew this would be a temporary arrangement. We were feeling restless. Dissatisfaction often precedes journeys towards change, building impetus to propel us towards the new. There was a draught blowing under the canvas as the guy ropes slackened, the flapping a repeated reminder that it was time to move on. We had a choice either to listen to the voice of reason and limp our way to the finishing line, or take to heart what we felt the Lord was indicating. Barry was sixty-two years old, but continued to have a fiery vision for ministry. Years of retirement did not bode well for our joint future, but if we were to move on, where would we go? The Muffins were showing signs of growing independence. They were increasingly feeling distanced from the painful effects of the past. Barry was continuing to lead weekends away, but the invitations had dwindled. More churches were learning to access the gifts of the Spirit and minister them themselves. The New Wine conferences had revolutionised the church communities who attended them. They were now also taking teams to churches local to them. It was good for us to have a time to adjust to this very different way of life before our next move to London. London was to be a unique place of learning for us and a happy change of location for the Muffins.

Again the Lord made His appeal through the prophet Isaiah, 'Enlarge the place of your tent, stretch your tent curtains wide, do not hold back' (Isaiah 54:2).

John Peters was one of the young leaders who had accompanied Barry to Siberia, to teach at the summer Bible school there. Barry had a strange prophetic word when they were travelling together. He said to John, 'Although I am leading you at the present time, there will be a time when I will be under your leadership.' John was not convinced. It was strange to us too, but when the call came we were prepared. It was London calling and John who extended the invitation to us to join the staff of his church in Onslow Square.

Verses about the city had been leaping out of the Scriptures for several months, including one from a psalm: 'He led them by a straight way to a city where they could settle' (Psalm 107:7). I had written it down in one of my red notebooks, believing it to be significant. Despite my love of the country, I felt a strange magnetic draw to London, a place infrequently visited, despite being only a few stops down the Metropolitan line.

John was already in negotiation with the diocese regarding a large church in central London where numbers had dwindled to a handful. He hoped to move his congregation into it. Eventually it had been agreed with the Bishop of London that he would become the new rector of St Mary's, Bryanston Square, when renovations were complete. We served on staff at St Paul's, Onslow Square, which would be a short-term place of worship while the building works got underway. It sounded exciting. We got ready for the move. John's personal assistant, Kim, exercised great patience in looking for a suitable house for a short-term let that would be suitable for us. Nothing came up.

Barry was loading the boot of the car outside our home one Tuesday, when Graham, a member of St Andrew's with a prophetic gifting, walked past on the way to the station and stopped to greet him.

'I was praying for you this morning, and the Lord said you would hear about the house two weeks today, early morning.'

He waved and went on his way. Two weeks later, early as predicted, we had a phone call from Kim to say a property had unexpectedly come up for rental, but we would have to come up to London immediately. The estate agent would only hold it until lunchtime. We dropped everything and left. The house was perfect. It was time to pack up, say good-bye to much-loved friends at St Andrew's, leave Wick Cottage and move to Hammersmith. This was to be our new home in London in easy travelling distance initially of St Paul's, Onslow Square, and then later of St Mary's, Bryanston Square.

Moving to London from suburban Chorleywood was like being transported to another planet, with 'yummy mummies' on bicycles pulling children in boxes on wheels, young men in suits clutching their mobiles in animated conversation with unseen persons, while stepping off pavements and dodging between traffic. Energy rose from the streets. Steaming cups of coffee in cartons were being churned out of cafés to boost adrenaline levels. Multicultural mixes of people jostled on pavements to gain ground in their race to destinations. Taxis swerved and edged towards theirs.

At St Mary's people were trained to bend to its unique culture. John knew how to gain the attention of the communication-savvy. Talks were given in a pithy self-deprecating way, the content of which were brutally honest in self-put-downs, celebrating the funniest aspects of our shared humanity, while emphasising the message of God's grace. Tuesday staff meetings were equally entertaining. John had keen antennae to pick up any idiosyncrasy in his staff and chose his moments to expose it. This led to a lot of friendly banter and enforced humbling. The more sensitive learned to keep their heads beneath the parapet. Being edgy and relevant was important to John. His sayings were legendary. My favourite was, 'A good teacher is a bad teacher who got better.' It could be translated to apply to many situations where people were nervous about stepping out into new ventures. We had much to learn from John and also Jenny, his wife. With her deep understanding of people, she was brilliant at managing tricky situations. Behind the scenes it was not difficult to imagine her wise counselling steering the boat away from choppy waters.

Tradition and convention had been banished from St Mary's vocabulary, along with books of Common Prayer. The latter caused a bit of a stir when some ecclesiastical dignitary came to speak and sought to frame his contribution in words from the 'book'. Dust rose from storage cupboards in a frantic search for one!

Believing the Lord had placed us in this strange environment, it was up to us to adapt, to make necessary changes and above all, to watch and learn. Prayer, for me, had always been key to turning round situations and making inroads into the new. I was eager to set up some prayer strategy in Hammersmith that could be replicated in different areas of London where other members of the church were living. The congregation was young at the time, hardly beyond 'youth club' age, and they lived and worked in areas throughout the city. Travelling was a way of life. Many lived in one part of London, worked in another and found their way to St Mary's, a church they chose for its relevance to them, in yet another. It was unreasonable to expect them to extend their journeys further. Perhaps it would be possible to set up 'prayer houses' where local people who worshipped at St Mary's could meet.

Barry and I made it known that people would be welcome to come to our home at 7am to pray, followed by breakfast, once a week. It was a start, and it gave us opportunity to get to know a few people in the area, but it was not feasible for pop-up prayer houses to replicate what we were doing. Accommodation for the young men and women we were getting to know was predominantly single rooms in houses shared with others who, like them, worked in the city, but were not necessarily churchgoers. Eventually Barry and I hosted meetings in the church in the evenings that were attended straight from the workplace. While the worship band set up for these evenings, people drifted in munching salads from boxes to stave off their hunger after demanding days in the city. They were wonderful young men and women, creative, spiritual and having insights well beyond their physical years.

My sadness was the ever-changing population within the church. It was difficult to know in whom it would be appropriate to invest time to take on leadership roles when the question was always looming, 'Would they still be around in six months' time?'

Brokenness was the hallmark of this young, creative generation. I had a growing conviction that I should set up a course to help address the inner pain many were experiencing. I did feel the Lord guiding me in this, especially in the selection of possible leaders to work with me. Together with them I wrote the 'Freedom' course, which addressed many of the key issues that repeatedly came up during times of ministry. The team were wonderful in their expertise and commitment. We planned and prayed together and always evaluated each course with a view to allowing it to evolve to be increasingly relevant to the needs that were arising. Prayer was central to everything we planned, with time given each week for ministry, as requested by those who were wrestling with particularly painful issues. As leaders we too were challenged to continue our own journey to wholeness.

John, who always had his finger on the pulse, brought to our attention the fact that we should be looking to buy a permanent home as retirement loomed. We had not given it a thought! But yes, where would we live when we could no longer rely on church accommodation? I love that passage in Scripture that casually mentions, 'As it turned out … ' It is recorded in the book of Ruth, when Ruth was sent out to glean. 'As it turned out, she was working in a field belonging to Boaz' (Ruth 2:3). Boaz was a relative of her late husband and good husband material for Ruth, and so began a romance that led to marriage and the birth of a son. If I added up all the 'As it turned out' moments in my life, it would be evidence enough that God is not only my guide, but is also deeply involved in my destiny. He does not always leave obvious footprints of His presence. It is impossible to anticipate where His paths will lead, but His stamp is there if we have eyes to see: 'His paths [are] beyond tracing out' (Romans 11:33).

Our next steps in finding a home to purchase were the result of many apparent coincidences that led back to the guiding and generous hand of the Lord. Remembering that the Holy Spirit speaks in whispers, glimpses and nudges, these small communications are not to be ignored. Israel's history was changed in a moment when Ruth chose to glean in the field of Boaz. It resulted in a genealogy that culminated in the birth of Jesus: 'Boaz [was] the father of Obed, whose mother was Ruth, Obed the father of Jesse, and Jesse the father of King David' (Matthew 1:5-6). The line of David continued: 'Jacob [was] the father of Joseph, the husband of Mary, and Mary was the mother of Jesus who is called the Messiah (Matthew 1:16).

My father, who was very elderly, was finding his house difficult to manage. He had just put in an offer for a small, warden-controlled flat nearby. 'As it turned out', he decided at that time to divide the proceeds of his house sale between my brother and me, and pay cash for his new home. It also happened that insurance policies invested in years before and forgotten came to maturity at the same time. It also 'turned out' that house prices had temporarily slumped. Consequently, to our surprise we could seriously consider buying a house. We looked everywhere. The affordable homes that were available were simply depressing or had tiny outdoor spaces. I was adamant that having a small garden was a non-negotiable necessity for survival in the city.

A few houses down from the road where we lived, a house was being totally renovated and divided into large flats. I expressed an interest in seeing this new development, not with a serious intention of buying, but out of mere curiosity. This was a Holy Spirit nudge! Barry and I had made friends with people who worked in the estate agent's office round the corner and they had the key. They said they would show us round. As we entered the garden flat, the Holy Spirit came on me so powerfully I could hardly breathe. Before even looking round the ground floor and basement area I knew that this was to be our home. It seemed utterly impossible, but here we are today in a home that has blessed us in every way, with a garden that I have been able to develop. Our finances just about stretched to make it possible when the last outstanding bill was taken care of by a friend of Barry's who generously forwarded what we needed in stamp duty to secure the property.

Barry was well past the expected age of retirement when he felt the time had come for him to step down from St Mary's. His passion for preaching and teaching were unabated. He would have to trust that opportunities beyond St Mary's would open up for him, and they did and continue to do so. I had been involved in counselling for many years and also believed it was something I was called to do. I have been able to continue to do this informally. These drives to minister just do not go away. Knowing what we are called to do motivates us throughout our lives. Paul spoke boldly about his calling: 'I am the apostle to the Gentiles, I take pride in my ministry' (Romans 11:13). I knew our future would unfold and would be used fruitfully. We would not simply be filling in time until the great call upwards.

Identifying our gifts and knowing our calling direct us towards a fulfilling future. It requires courage and determination to pursue goals that will get us where we want to be. Inner pain distorts the vision that we need to hold before us to push through. Combating self-doubt fuelled by low expectations was one of my biggest battles. Coming through it was like coming into a wide open space. This is what is promised us when we push forward to eradicate the taunting voice of darkness. 'He brought me out into a spacious place; he rescued me because he delighted in me' (Psalm 18:19).

A surprise call from a friend gave immediate direction to the beginning of this new season. He had noted that Barry had been around fifty years in Christian ministry and felt that this should be celebrated by a holiday. Consequently, we found ourselves in the West Indies, returning to London five weeks later. This time away proved to be pivotal in shaping Barry's present preaching ministry. Vivid prophecies regarding the end times rocked his inner life and impressed upon him an urgency to communicate the message of salvation whenever opportunities arose. He tested this out day after day, on sun-drenched West Indian islands. Whenever an opening was presented he sowed a seed, believing that these small plantings had the power to generate life.

Back home, invitations to speak came from surprising sources and these too were used to convey the message burning in his heart. I meanwhile had joined a local group of women who met to pray. They have proved to be precious and supportive friends. A growing number of speaking engagements have also come my way. People continue to visit and in a way life is not very different from before, apart from the fact that we have a greater choice in deciding how we use our time. Rather than feeling we are 'over the hill', we feel we are still mountain climbing, taking years of ministry experience with us while learning new truths every day.

Working with people of very different personalities has broadened our horizons and taught us a wisdom we would never have known. Our time with the wonderful young people of St Mary's and the unique leadership of John had opened our eyes to the 'today' generation. It was a great privilege to work with them and we made lasting friendships.

Chapter 10
Time of Testing

I liked being in my sixties. It still had a youthful hint about it. That awful 'old age' label was far enough away to be pushed into the back of a drawer and dismissed. My seventieth birthday, therefore, crept up on me unawares. October was drawing near again and there were calls from the family to think about a celebration. Something small, I decided, a lunch with friends and an evening with the family in a London restaurant.

A kind young friend and budding chef from the church volunteered to cook a celebratory meal for me at home – an offer I could not refuse. Ten good friends and Barry sat around our dining room table joining with me in acknowledging another milestone of my life. I was so glad they were there. Barry and I had received unsettling news the week before.

Barry had suffered a few bouts of abdominal discomfort. Our GP did not think there was anything to worry about, but being conscientious he arranged a few tests, all of which came back negative. To be doubly sure, he arranged for an appointment with a colorectal consultant at St Mary's Hospital, Paddington. He also did not think there was anything to worry about, but agreed to organise a further test. I accompanied Barry to the clinic, savouring the opportunity to read in the waiting room while he had his colonoscopy, a procedure that normally takes around half an hour.

An hour had passed and icy fingers of doubt gripped me. I was summoned by one of the medical team.

A cancerous tumour had been discovered in the wall of the descending colon of the large bowel. Barry, who was lying on a stretcher, looked diminished and frail. The news had clearly been a shock to him too. Kindness mixed with realistic reassurance was relayed through the medical team. They were confident that the tumour could be successfully removed. Appointments were made to see the team who would operate at the end of October and a specialist nurse was assigned to answer any questions we might have. She gave us preliminary information and promised to phone the next day to answer any other queries.

We returned to Hammersmith in a daze. I phoned the family to tell them the news. Barry and I talked all day and wrote down questions to ask our assigned nurse. I felt as if I had received a body blow; celebrating a birthday was the last thing I felt like doing.

However, having loving friends with us was just what we needed. It did not feel awkward. No one felt they had to be guarded in what they said. We chatted as always, sharing information we had received from the hospital, interspersed with the usual banter, ridiculous stories and jokes that mark friendships that have stood the test of time. They gathered round us before leaving and prayed with an assurance that all would be well. We felt confident too, but we were entering an unpredictable season.

Ominous clouds of uncertainty were building on the horizon, threatening our ordered rhythm of life. They caused an emotional upheaval in Barry. Events were moving too quickly for him. He did not have time to process them. It made him anxious. Reassurance is only helpful if it is based on certainty and we did not have that. Putting a strategy in place to build coping mechanisms was urgent.

We began the day with prayer and meditation on a psalm, meeting again to pray mid-morning. We closed the day with prayer too and thankfully Barry slept well. The anxiety did not go away, but there were footholds to keep him steady.

Bad news is what it is, and you cannot magically make it good. A shadow had passed over us, separating us from the life that we had known. There was no certainty that it would be recovered. Scriptures have stood the test of time, putting strength into those who have taken them into frail hearts. We grabbed them greedily and found that same sustaining power. It was important to hold on and not give way to fear.

Our friend Liz invited us to join her and a mutual friend, Val, for coffee at a hotel in a nearby village. I remembered it from the past as being a superb place to dine. Despite the advancing of autumn, we sat outside at a table in the garden in bright sunshine and drank our coffee from pretty bone-china cups. To our surprise, Liz rummaged deep in her bag and brought out a notebook. She had been praying and felt God had given her a word for us. The essence of it was that we would find favour, because God was with us. It was a powerful word and proved true. It was fulfilled at every step.

Val, who had sat quietly listening as Liz gave her word, suddenly delved into her bag and brought out a bottle of anointing oil. Quoting familiar words from James that we had used many times before, she anointed Barry: 'Is anyone among you ill? Let them call the elders of the church to pray over them and anoint them with oil in the name of the Lord. And the prayer offered in faith will make the sick person well; the Lord will raise them up' (James 5:14-15).

Prayers were made. I am not sure that either Liz or Val would have described themselves as elders, but their ministry was precious to us. Often, in darker moments, we thought back to that time and drew strength from it – and some amusement. Other guests at the hotel gave us some strange looks as they took discreet glances in our direction. They would certainly have had their own theories about what they had witnessed!

A date for surgery had been fixed for the end of October. We packed in as many outings as possible before the date. One day, using our National Trust passes we visited Ham House, the former home of the Duke of Lauderdale. When we reached the duchess' private sitting room a pleasant lady, who had been observing us with interest, stepped forward to speak to Barry.

'Do you remember that we sat together in the waiting room at the outpatients' department of St Mary's Hospital yesterday?' she asked.

The coincidence was extraordinary. How could a complete stranger be spirited from a hospital waiting room in central London to a historical building by the river in Ham to coincide with our visit the following day? It was a sign to us, boosting our faith and confirming that God could do anything.

Barry's operation was successfully performed. He woke with a stoma that he had not anticipated. It had been suggested that this might happen and Barry had been offered some counselling by the stoma team to prepare him in advance of the operation, but he did not want to think about it, believing that it would just not happen. He was wrong. It did, and he hated it. It made him feel unclean and vulnerable. When he was well enough to go out for a short trip to Richmond in the car, he became agitated if there was not a toilet facility nearby. I had to plan routes to include one.

Chemotherapy treatment was started at the end of November under the supervision of the oncology team at Charing Cross, our local hospital and a wing of Imperial College. Unstoppable waves rose and broke. Psalm 23, so familiar, so timeless, took the brunt of the force. The shadow of death came dangerously close as the chemicals invaded Barry's body. Huge toxic doses of destructive elements were building inside him. He went into kidney failure. The emergency team at Charing Cross worked hard to flush them out. I waited anxiously.

Barry recalled the terrible darkness that descended upon him as he slipped in and out of consciousness. Repeated nightmares of clinging to a high wall by his fingertips tormented him. As strength ebbed from his fingers, the fall seemed inevitable, then he would awaken again. Later a kindly consultant confided cheerfully, 'We nearly lost you.'

Recovery was a slow journey. Every part of Barry's integrated being was in shock. His emotions and mind had yet to catch up with the trauma he had experienced. Days spent in a hospital bed felt like a painful exile. He was desperate to come home. A troubled man in a neighbouring bed was persistently calling out. He was abusive to the staff and also his wife, who patiently sat with him and tried to calm him. Noonie spoke to the staff and asked if he could be moved. His behaviour was having a destructive effect on the other patients in the ward. She later negotiated for Barry to come home. He was not really well enough, but I promised diligent care and it was agreed. Barry's relief was palpable. Home, his own bed: he had dreamed of them.

My respect for Job, that tormented ancient, whose grim story is recorded before the book of Psalms, has grown. Satan's evil cunning is put into action to destroy everything that humanly speaking Job could have relied upon, in tests to break his faith; multiple losses of both loved ones and property were followed by a tormenting skin disease. Job proved to be a formidable opponent. He steadfastly clung to eternal truths he had discovered in his walk with God.

Long before other prophetic announcements were made about One who would come to save us, Job appears to have had unusual insight. He describes an advocate in heaven, who made intercessions to God on his behalf. Job refers to Him as his friend: 'Even now my witness is in heaven; my advocate is on high. My intercessor is my friend as my eyes pour out tears to God; on behalf of a man he pleads with God as one pleads with a friend' (Job 16:19-21). This 'friend' in heaven has unique power to redeem. Job foresaw that He would one day at the end of all time come to earth. He speaks with conviction about Him: 'I know that my redeemer lives, and that in the end he will stand on the earth' (Job 19:25). Job is utterly convinced of this: 'After my skin has been destroyed, yet in my flesh I will see God; I myself will see him with my own eyes – I, and not another. How my heart yearns within me!' (Job 19:26-27).

Life on earth is transient, but if we know and trust Jesus, eternity and a new body awaits us in the end!

The word I clung to was also in the book of Job: 'I will wait for my renewal to come' (Job 14:14). Renewal seemed far off, but inside I felt it would come. I knew Barry would be reunited with the 'self' he had temporarily been separated from.

Barry and I had advantages not afforded to Job. We had wonderful family, friends and neighbours. Job's friends were convinced that God was punishing him. They sought solutions to his plight and goaded him to face up to his failings. In long rallies of arguments they batted back and forth, until Job cried out, 'You are miserable comforters, all of you!' (Job 16:2). He longed for them to be quiet.

Not once did those closest to us venture to suggest either reasons for or solutions to our plight. They simply expressed kindness. Sometimes they sat quietly with Barry, who drew strength from them being there.

Behind the scenes in the book of Job lurked the heartless figure of Satan. God wipes the smile off his face by bringing restoration to Job, who learned a few lessons on the way. He was further enlightened and his faith was strengthened.

There were yet more battles for Barry to face. His initial discharge from Charing Cross was short-lived, just one day! During the night his temperature rose, his breathing became laboured and he was coughing up mucus. I phoned our son Bruce who worked at Great Ormond Street Hospital. He came over immediately and our next-door neighbour dropped everything to take us back to Charing Cross. Another week of drips, medication and oxygen followed. To my amusement, as a concession to the festive season, a small loop of red crêpe paper had been attached to the arched entrance to the bay where Barry had his bed.

Before Barry was finally discharged, Jonnie, our son-in-law, helped me to put up a Christmas tree in the lounge. I wanted our home to look festive and welcoming for such an important season. Our lovely family visited in small batches and on Christmas Day, those who could make it crossed the local green to the pub to enjoy a Christmas lunch. While Barry sat on the sofa sipping that

Jewish cure-all, chicken soup, we tucked in to a five-course meal!

The horror of what Barry had experienced bound him to the event for months afterwards. He could not shake himself free, going over and over it like a mantra and finding no immediate resolution to the darkness that had invaded him. How was it possible to make sense of such an ugly intrusion into his body – and soul?

Darkness and light battled it out on the right-hand side of the sofa where Barry sat each day in weakness, while kind visitors came and went. They left loving deposits of reassurance, made prayers for God's intervention and brought snippets of news from the outside world to engage him.

Sofa-time was interspersed with hospital appointments, always involving blood tests, sometimes scans. Explanations were given for the potentially lethal reaction to chemotherapy and reassurances made that no more would be given. Indeed, there was no need, the cancer showed no signs of recurrence. A final operation was planned to reverse the plumbing of the bowel, necessitated during the first operation. This was done to preserve the operation site from harmful bacteria. I feared the impact of this on Barry's fragile state.

To my surprise, he made an excellent recovery, seeming to wake up from his exile to another world. His appetite improved, healing of his considerable wound accelerated and he decided he no longer needed me to drive him three times a week to the local surgery, but would walk there. Our short length of privet hedge at the front of the house, which had been dormant through the winter months, was beginning to sprout new growth again. Barry began the task of giving it a trim, helped by our neighbour who stuffed the cuttings into a black, plastic bag. This did, of course, exhaust Barry, but gave him the satisfaction of knowing that strength was returning.

When you have been very ill, it is difficult to believe that life as you have known it will ever return again. Those who have suffered similarly bring hope when they testify to eventual restoration. 'You will come through this!' – wonderful words given from personal experience, bringing shafts of light into the grim world of sickness. But what of the darkness: is anything gained? Perhaps what is difficult to understand is that the ill and the well are indeed in two different worlds. There is no meeting point. We cannot enter their world and they cannot enter ours. In the bleakest days, Barry was unreachable. I could only allow the daily routines of care to speak to him for me.

Happily, spring began to break through. Renewal, growth, colour, regeneration brought their own message. I was thankful for the investment of time given to planting in the autumn. We peered through the patio doors daily to view the results of my labour.

By mid-June the darkness had permanently lifted; our period of house arrest was over. Barry was anxious to cast off his ill persona and get on with life. However, he did want to formulate what he felt God had shown him. On Saturday afternoon, the Glastonbury weekend, when the customary heavy showers caused festival-goers to don their Wellington boots, we sat down in the lounge with sheets of paper to evaluate the past months. It was good to feel we could.

Our conclusions were that darkness and evil are realities in the spiritual world. Doors were opened to prowling demons when we engaged with fear. Fear is the enemy of the soul, separating us from truth and firing our imagination with pictures of doom. Prayer keeps these cunning forces at bay. Jesus tells Peter: 'Simon, Simon, Satan has asked to sift all of you as wheat. But I have prayed for you, Simon, that your faith may not fail' (Luke 22:31-32).

When circumstances are overwhelming it is hard to engage with the Lord in ways we have known before. Having family and friends to take this commitment up for us held us together. Throughout the long months we felt daily undergirded. Hope took a firm stand against fear. Prophetic words and pictures were given us that we could hold on to. People who were strangers to each other offered similar messages, confirming that Barry would be healed. He would have to trust that opportunities beyond St Mary's would open up for him, and they did and continue to do so.

Light is a reality. It was evident in those who visited, sometimes from long distances. The light in them reflected what we knew: Christ is in those who believe. There is no greater power. Jesus proclaimed, 'I am the light of the world' (John 8:12). Darkness is not able to put out that light.

What of Job? There was a showdown when the Lord eventually had His voice. He set a few things straight. He is Almighty God, Creator of the universe; who are we to demand an accounting of Him? Job was humbled before Him. Eliphaz, Zophar and Bildad, those miserable friends, made sacrifices and Job prayed to God for them. His prayer was accepted by the Lord. It all turned out well in the end. Job is given twice as much as he had before. I am not sure if he had a new wife. There is scant reference to his old one who confessed that Job's bad breath was a bit of a turn-off (Job 19:17)!

Chapter 11
The Wonders

Before the days draw in I like to do as many of the outdoor jobs as the unpredictable weather allows. This involves the late planting of bulbs, the trimming back of straggly bushes and a last forking over of the flowerbeds. When I have done all that I can to leave my small outdoor space in order, I like to look at what I have done and reflect on it with satisfaction. It's permissible to do this. Satisfaction is the reward for doing the best you can do. Solomon himself says that it is appropriate that we should enjoy this small reward for our labour. (However, he does sound a bit miserable in the expression of his conclusions!) 'It is appropriate for a person to eat, to drink and to find satisfaction in their toilsome labour under the sun during the few days of life God has given them' (Ecclesiastes 5:18).

God also looked at all He had created and not only found satisfaction, but pleasure. He 'saw that it was good' (see Genesis 1:10, 12, 18, 21, 25, 31). In my heart I echo this as I close the doors and give my attention to other pursuits.

It is good to finish well, whatever we are doing. Completing a task gives us a sense of accomplishment. Jesus, having done what He had come to do, proclaimed from the cross, 'It is finished' (John 19:30). He had won the battle for the souls of humankind. This was in fulfilment of the Father's wishes as set out in the Scriptures. Before giving up His Spirit, He had a last taster of life on earth, wine mixed with myrrh. Jesus and His Father had talked about His final battle for the redemption of the souls of the fallen as 'drinking the cup'. It was a terrible cup to drink and Jesus agonised about the consequences, crying out to the Father: 'My Father, if it is possible, may this cup be taken from me. Yet not as I will, but as you will' (Matthew 26:39).

There was no other way. Looking ahead, He knew He would be reunited with the unsullied world of the kingdom of God in heaven, when His task had been accomplished on the cross. Later I can imagine Jesus and His Father sitting together reminiscing on the extraordinary journey Jesus had taken from heaven to earth to bring salvation to humankind.

One of the pleasures at the end of a year is to look back and recall the standout events that have impacted us. Barry and I like to do this. It is good to stop and remember. These times of reflection cement such moments in our memories, the truths gained, the pleasure received from them continuing to shape our future. God, who is constantly drawing us towards His good purposes for us, also asks us to stop and reflect, and remember what He has done. His many acts of faithfulness can be blurred by the momentum of the present if we do not take time to recall them. King David reminds us of this when he says, 'Remember the wonders he has done' (1 Chronicles 16:12).

It is not difficult to recognise the unique power of God that gives Him the right to be called the God of wonders. The wonders are all round us for us to see. Paul, writing in Romans, simply implores them to look at the world around them: 'Since the creation of the world God's invisible qualities – his eternal power and divine nature – have been clearly seen, being understood from what has been made, so that people are without excuse' (Romans 1:20).

Being a woman of the soil, I have regularly been privy to these wonders as I have dug, planted, watered and watched. It amazes me that small, hard, brown seeds, planted in season, have such life within them that they can burgeon into plants exploding with colour. Can this small dried-up seed really have so much power within it to burst into the plant featured on the seed packet? Hedgerows and wide expanses of woodlands beyond the structured world of my garden do exactly the same. In season, they too burst into colours of all shades and grow to huge dimensions. They yield fruit and blossom with little human intervention. I need to engage with this world of beauty when my inner life becomes a desert. God whispers to me in these moments, 'You have ceased to wonder. I want you to discover Me again as the God of wonders.'

In earlier days my daily walk with my dog, Sophie, took me to the common in Chorleywood, just a few hundred metres from our home. These walks were like a step out in companionship with the Lord – I felt He was pointing out the smallest details of creation as we walked together. They were among the most precious memories of my time in Chorleywood. I loved the tall grasses of delicate purples that rippled like silk in the breeze; the smell of gorse in early spring, a light, sweet coconut fragrance; pink buds bursting to light green leaves on the oak trees; the dew on the grass in the morning; ponds laced with green weed and popping with water life; clouds of pink, springy heather; the sunshine yellow of coffee-scented broom; the red-spotted toadstools in autumn; rabbits retreating to their burrows; acorns crunching underfoot; the fresh, cool air of a new day; blackberries dripping from thorny stems; squirrels hopping in loops; holly resplendent with berries; the sombre yew; logs scattered beneath the trees; the snap of sticks as I walked; jays calling; paths pressed firmed by decades of feet and winding through woodlands; light piercing branches; old man's beard trailing through hedges.

Sometimes in my wild imaginings I gather together a group of eminent international scientists. There is to be an examination and they can all work together. They have four hours to complete the task. The brief is outlined: 'All you are being asked to do this morning is to make an apple, just a simple dessert apple, any variety you choose, starting now.' Hmm!

Praise erupts spontaneously from the heart in the unveiling of wonders. They continue to feed the soul and capture the imagination. God asks us, 'What do you see?' I hate those barren times when I see nothing. My response then is like the reading on a barometer of my soul that registers an inner winter. 'Remember the wonders,' He whispers.

Remembering the wonders ignites again the life that uniquely flows from the Spirit of God. He is both the Creator and the redeemer, bringing the new and reclaiming the old. He is the God of the impossible. How is it possible for God to take broken, damaged lives and put them together to live purposefully in relationship with Him and others? It is a glorious mystery. To know that do I have purpose not only here on earth, but in a promised eternal kingdom in the future, is incomprehensible. Jesus did this for me. It did not stop there. There was more to come. He has given me a continuing resource of power to help me day by day. All I have to do is access it.

I was thinking about this one morning when Barry and I met for our daily prayer time. A picture of a large round metal platter came to mind. It nearly filled the room where we were sitting. On it was a huge loaf of bread. Recalling the Lord's Prayer and the words, 'Give us today our daily bread' (Matthew 6:11), it was clear that this particular loaf would be greatly in excess of my daily needs. What did I need, that I could take from this bread? Well, strength – I was feeling a bit weary; break off a piece … inspiration for a talk I was preparing; break off another piece … anxiety about a family member; take some more … Jesus claims that He is 'the bread of life' (John 6:35). All I have to do is take what I need for each day. John, in his Gospel, recalls another message Jesus told the listening crowd: 'I have come that they may have life, and have it to the full' (John 10:10). What did He mean by this 'life'? Well, He was certainly not speaking to dead people. He was speaking to living ones! Simply stated, Jesus meant that He had a lot more to offer than they already had. That is super-abundant life, over and above anything they had known before. They, and we only have to ask and take. Jesus is willing to share with us what He has. The power that emanates from Him will always be over and above what we need. Paul was turned upside down by it.

As Saul, he was like an angry bull charging towards the Christian community to destroy it. It was an offence to his law-abiding code of life to bring a message of grace that could be received by faith in Jesus. It was outrageous. Religious observance, as he understood it as a Pharisee, demanded the hard grind of keeping to relentless practices in adherence to Jewish law, and he was going to ensure that others in the Jewish community did this too. God had other ideas.

Setting an ambush for Saul on the Damascus Road, God met with him. Saul was blinded by a heavenly light, and challenged by a voice – the risen Lord Jesus Himself. It changed everything. Leaving his past behind, Saul – now called Paul – fully embraced what he had once considered to be heretical teachings. Filled with the Holy Spirit, he was empowered to speak the gospel fearlessly to the very people, the religious Jews, whose way of life he had been defending. Later he preached this same message to the Gentile community whom he had believed to be beyond redemption. Paul testifies to the great power that motivates his ministry: 'I strenuously contend with all the energy Christ so powerfully works in me'

(Colossians 1:29). He became so much more than he could ever have been humanly speaking. What had happened to him? We know the sort of person he was, driven by the requirements of the law as a Pharisee; he had simply been transformed by a mighty 'power from on high' (see Luke 24:49) – heavenly power.

I know with certainty that spiritual power is available to help me live out this life on earth. When I engage with this truth I feel hopeful, expectant, believing that the good that flows from the kingdom of God will flow to me. I know in my heart God sees me as more than I am. My life has endless possibilities with His power at work within me. Also, I not only know the sort of person I was, but who I can be. God has been working to change me into that person. With His power, I can become so much more. Filled up like a balloon with the good Spirit of God, I can look kindly at people, love them, want to pray for them, want them to be blessed. I can look at the marginalised and those who are oppressed. I can have a heightened awareness of what God wants me to do. I want all this and know that I can get it. I simply have to ask. I want Him to continue to bring changes. I want to be the one saying with confidence that it is God's mighty power at work within me.

It seems that God does not want us to be 'ordinary'. He sees the potential that He has placed within us to be so much more. Paul rebukes the Corinthians for acting like 'mere humans' (1 Corinthians 3:3). We do not have to slide into our basic feral nature. There is a greater power to help us.

The kingdom of God is near us. It is an unseen world, but no less of a reality. Although living on earth, this other kingdom is constantly breaking in to help us. As believers we are, because of our faith, repeatedly making transitions from this world to the next. It is natural and authentic for us to do so. It is possibly strange to others. This is not an imaginary world like Narnia, where we enter a wardrobe into a winter wonderland. It is a reality we engage with and receive strength from. The unseen world of the Spirit is at the heart of Jesus' teachings. It is a wonder.

These transitions in no way annul our humanity, which is clearly in evidence, especially as we get older. Too often, perhaps, those of us more senior in years obsess about our physical health. The sluggishness of our bowels, the diminishing ability to 'get around', our memory lapses and eroding joints dominate our conversations. But the fact is, we are getting ready for the final transition when we will leave our ailing bodies behind, like a discarded outer casing of a chrysalis, to receive new ones, spiritual bodies for a spiritual kingdom: the ultimate wonder. On earth we are integrated beings, but it is the Spirit who brings added life to us. He – that is, the Spirit – was Jesus' parting gift to His followers: 'You will receive power when the Holy Spirit comes on you' (Acts 1:8). The Holy Spirit arrived as promised! He is the stamp, the evidence of our union with Christ.

Underestimating His power to intervene and bring change saddens the One who came to do those very things. Our hardness of heart can obstruct Him from working. During His time on earth, Jesus strongly confronted those who did this. Standing before the congregation in the synagogue on the Sabbath He noticed a man with a shrivelled hand. He asked those present: 'Which is lawful on the Sabbath: to do good or to do evil, to save life or to kill?' (Mark 3.4). They refused to respond. This distressed Him. He healed the man and the religious and other leaders plotted how they might kill Jesus. Our own actions and the silting up of our hearts are what let us down repeatedly and obstruct the work of the Holy Spirit.

Building our faith in Jesus by being willing to respond to the Holy Spirit's promptings will be a lifelong challenge for us, His followers.

God can do anything. Nothing is beyond His power. This truth was underlined to me when travelling in New Zealand on a Faith-Sharing mission to the South and North Islands with Barry and our friends Arthur and Shirley. God spoke to me in the strangest of ways and through a tiny jellyfish. On a warm afternoon we stopped off to swim in one of the inlets in Marlborough Sounds. The water was crystal-clear and Barry was the first to dive in while we watched from the shoreline. He was not on his own. Small, harmless jellyfish were bobbing around in the water. Barry gently lifted one out and waded with it to the shore to show us. He placed it on the shingle, where it flopped into a shapeless blob. Scooping it back up he returned it to the water and it swam off. This picture repeated itself again and again in my thoughts and I meditated on it throughout the day. God does this sometimes to unfold the message He wants us to hear. We need to give it time to seep through. The message came in the strangest of ways. An underwater scenario stirred in my imagination, of the little jellyfish returning to its shoal and relating to them the strange adventure it had had.

It says, 'You'll never guess what happened to me today.'

'No, what happened?'

'I was swimming around and suddenly I came up out of the water, through the air and I found myself on the beach. I stayed there, unable to move for a period of time. Then I was transported through the air a second time and found myself back in the water again.'

'Ha, ha! That is ridiculous and totally impossible. We don't believe you.'

The picture fades as God speaks. 'It was nothing for Barry to stretch out his arm, lift that jellyfish into air and onto the beach and back again. It was effortless and only took a moment. For the jellyfish on its own it would be totally impossible and incomprehensible to raise itself from the water. It was not equipped to do it. I can do anything. All I have to do is stretch out My hand. I can change a situation in a moment. Nothing is impossible for Me. Do you believe this?'

God is God. He proves this time and time again, not least by masterminding the great exodus from Egypt: 'Has any god ever tried to take for himself one nation out of another nation, by testings, by signs and wonders, by war, by a mighty hand and an outstretched arm, or by great and awesome deeds, like all the things the LORD your God did for you in Egypt before your very eyes? You were shown these things so that you might know that the LORD is God' (Deuteronomy 4:34-35).

Humanly impossible situations present themselves regularly. There are no reasonable solutions to them. The wonders are there for us to remember that there is a God in heaven for whom all things are possible. The memory of the jellyfish has repeatedly strengthened my faith to turn the impossible into prayer. Wonders lead to worship, which leads us into the presence of God and into the unseen world of the Spirit. This validates our faith. God appeals to us through the wonders, calling us to open our eyes and see: 'Stop and consider God's wonders' (Job 37:14); 'Remember the wonders he has done' (1 Chronicles 16:12).

God, who is intimately involved with our lives, longs to reveal His wonders through what we see, through answered prayers, and the daily guidance He gives. He speaks through visions, dreams, pictures and above all, the Scriptures; these inspired writings bring revelation of the kingdom of God that is near us, yet unseen. We are encouraged to be bounty-hunters, seeking for the treasure, the mysteries and the secrets of the kingdom of God. They are all available to us to discover. Jesus confirms this: 'The knowledge of the secrets of the kingdom of heaven has been given to you' (Matthew 13:11).

John, writing his gospel message, testifies to what he has discovered and observed during his time with Jesus. It did not finish at the death of Jesus. John's encounters with the unseen world of the Spirit continued even into old age, when imprisoned on the Greek island of Patmos. Heaven broke into his isolation, revealing the mysteries of an unseen world in which he would shortly be a resident.

He always knew there was much more. The last verse of John's Gospel states: 'Jesus did many other things as well. If every one of them were written down, I suppose that even the whole world would not have room for the books that would be written' (John 21:25).

In chronicling some of the life-changing events I have experienced, I also know there will be many more, and hope before the door of October Cottage finally closes to record as many as possible. There is a small bundle of empty red notebooks, yet to be filled. I look forward with anticipation to filling them!

Biography

Mary Kissell trained as a nurse and clinical nurse teacher. She lives in Hammersmith with her husband, Barry, and shares her passion for 'writing it down' with other notebook-scribblers and list-keepers.